Lance Parkin

The Pocket Essential

ALAN MOORE

www.pocketessentials.com

First published in Great Britain 2001 by Pocket Essentials, 18 Coleswood Road, Harpenden, Herts, AL5 1EQ

Distributed in the USA by Trafalgar Square Publishing, PO Box 257, Howe Hill Road, North Pomfret, Vermont 05053

A CIP catalogue record for this book is available from the British Library.

ISBN 1-903047-70-6

2 4 6 8 10 9 7 5 3 1

Book typeset by Pdunk
Printed and bound by Cox & Wyman

Acknowledgements

Thanks to Allan Bednar, Simon Bucher-Jones, Graeme Burk, Paul Castle, Mark Clapham, Steve Holland, Mark Jones, Greg McElhatton, Jim Smith and Paul Duncan.

Special thanks to Alan Moore for reading the manuscript, and for his kind comments.

CONTENTS

1. Alan Moore Knows The Score

Alan Moore is the best writer of comic books there has ever been.

That's a bold statement and it's not one that's meant to demean the efforts of many others who have worked in the medium. There have been more prolific and more commercially successful writers. There have been writers who have created characters that are household names. But there have been no writers who have worked so well in so many different genres, whose work has moved the form into new literary and artistic areas, garnered so much critical praise, or whose work is so eagerly anticipated.

Moore's closest rival by those criteria is Grant Morrison, author of *The Invisibles* and *New X-Men*. Morrison has written some wonderful series, is consistently versatile and inventive, but while his work on the long-running series *Animal Man, Doom Patrol, The Invisibles* demonstrate he's exceptionally talented, he has yet to lay down landmark graphic novels like Moore.

There have been other works with a claim to be the best comic book: Frank Miller's *Dark Knight Returns*, Katsuhiro Otomo's *Akira*, Neil Gaiman's *The Sandman*, Jodorowsky and Moebius' *The Incal*, Bryan Talbot's *The Adventures Of Luther Arkwright* or Art Spiegelman's *Maus*, among others. But their writers have tended not to be prolific, or their other work has failed to demonstrate the sheer variety and depth of Moore's.

So, let's do the list: Among many other things, major and minor, Alan Moore has written *The Ballad Of Halo Jones*, *Watchmen*, *Marvelman* (known in the United States as *Miracleman*), *V For Vendetta*, *Swamp Thing*, 'Whatever Happened To The Man Of Tomorrow?', *The League Of Extraordinary Gentlemen*, *The Killing Joke*, *Supreme* and *From Hell*. Ten stories, ranging from long runs in weekly or monthly comics, through limited series to one-off specials. But all of the above have a good claim for a place on anyone's 'best of' list. Taken together, it's simply an unrivalled body of work.

Moore is also an important figure in the recent history of comics. He was the first comics writer living in Britain to do prominent work in America. Since the mid-eighties, following in Moore's footsteps, a whole wave of writers and artists have crossed the Atlantic to work on some of the real icons of American popular culture. Nowadays, if you pick up a superhero comic from the States, there's a good chance it's written or drawn by someone from the UK. The other thing that distinguished Moore in the early eighties was that he was famous solely for his writing, rather than as a writer/artist (just as many acclaimed cinema directors are actually writer/directors). Moore manages to be an auteur in the medium without drawing – an achievement in itself.

Alan Moore was born in Northampton in 1953, to working-class parents (his father, Ernest, worked in a brewery, his mother, Sylvia, at a printer's). He still lives in Northampton, and the town often features in his fiction. He avidly read British comics like *Topper* and *Beezer*, and when he was seven he discovered his first American comics (*Flash*, *Detective Comics* and other DC titles) on a market stall. In the sixties, American comics were widely distributed in Britain as importers bought up unsold stock and returns cheaply, and Moore soon discovered *Fantastic Four #3* and was a regular Marvel reader of whatever titles became available, the distribution system being imperfect. Some weeks that would mean Atlas monster books. On bad weeks it would be *Caspar The Friendly Ghost*. It was an eclectic mix, and he clearly has a lot of affection for the comics of his childhood because they have formed the foundation for a lot of his work.

Four types of comics in particular have been clear influences. When Moore was very young, horror comics were a focus for parental outrage on both sides of the Atlantic. In particular, those published by EC were full of gruesome violence – beheadings, disfigurements and the like. In Britain the *Eagle* was launched as a moral counterpoint to them. In America the Comics Code Authority was set up to regulate the industry. Superheroes like Superman, Batman and Captain Marvel were more wholesome, and these have been the staple of the industry since the late thirties. While Britain has never embraced superheroes, preferring more straightforward science fiction characters like Dan Dare or Judge Dredd, there were a few British superheroes, like Marvelman, and these tended to mix science fiction and fantasy motifs with the more straightforward heroics. At the age of 15 Moore was still reading mainstream comics from a wide variety of companies like Charlton, who published a slightly more politically sophisticated type of superhero, and ACG, enjoying them all. At the same time he was discovering underground comix and magazines that fell between those and the mainstream: Wally Wood's *Witzend* and Bill Spicer's *Graphic Story Magazine*, which reprinted Will Eisner's Spirit and which Moore considers the best comics fanzine ever. These titles were influential at a time – by now the late sixties – when Moore was discovering the early days of British comics fandom and was exposed to EC titles, MAD Comics reprints and the work of William Burroughs and the Beat writers in America and home-grown counter-culture magazines like *Oz*.

Comics have always represented a subculture – one with its own language and role models, and a sense of its own history and myth. Names like Will Eisner, Harvey Kurtzman and Jack Kirby, meaningless to outsiders, are held in awe. The letters pages and fanzines have codified an unfolding history of comics and, as some titles have been in continuous publication for sixty years or more, it is possible to trace developments and changing tastes over generations. Naturally, all sorts of narrative conventions and traditions have evolved. The comics industry is insular and its main subject matter is comics itself – endless reiterations of characters' narrative history, and a self-sustaining mythology of a 'golden age' in the past. Adult readers are encouraged to view comics as limited edition pieces of art. Price guides often start with ten-page descriptions of exactly what sort of plastic bag comics should be kept in, which cardboard boxes and even which way up comics should be stored. Moore has always had an uneasy relationship with this. In one of his first published stories, 'Profits Of Doom,' a short one-off strip in the *Eagle*, a comic collector rips off someone selling him a rare '50s horror comic, but gets his come-uppance when the comic comes to life and kills him. It's a simple tale, and one that doesn't need an in-depth knowledge of comics history, but Moore has that knowledge and knows many of his readers will. A lot of Moore's work is concerned with the history of comics – subverting it, redefining it, challenging it, or often just celebrating it. It's the medium he's interested in: the form, how to tell stories with it and the subject matter. He recognises the iconic power of comic strips – archetypal battles between good and evil – but clearly feels they can be put to better use than they have been in the past.

Throughout his career, Moore has returned to the most iconic superhero of all – Superman. Superman stories are fertile ground for Moore. Superman has been the backbone character for the industry for over sixty years and one of the great icons of the twentieth century, recognised around the world. Most people can describe the basic set-up: the man who's strong, who can fly, who wears his pants on the outside and who works in a big city at a newspaper with the woman he loves. It's a myth rooted in the real world, but one that's a childish fantasy.

Time and again, Alan Moore has told Superman stories. In the early eighties, he wrote *Marvelman*, which was about a Superman in the real world, where the normal rules of comics didn't apply. In these stories things changed and people died. The approach Moore adopted on *Marvel-*

man would help start a revolution. It would make Superman into an anachronism, and by 1986 would lead to a more realistic revamp of Superman himself. Fifty years of history were streamlined or, if it was felt to be too childish, just erased. Ironically, it was Moore who told the last old-style Superman story, 'Whatever Happened To The Man Of Tomorrow?', and it had more power and poignancy than just about any Superman story told before or since. There was a real sense of regret as Moore closed one chapter of the character's life. There was a palpable sense of loss as the supporting cast of playful childhood companions, superdogs and magical imps were put to the sword. Ten years later, with the new Superman sensibly married to Lois, with Lex Luthor a corporate player rather than a mad scientist, Moore's work on Superman rip-off *Supreme* was almost an act of atonement, as he lovingly recreated every last absurdity of the old-style Superman, and made them work for a modern audience. Then, as the millennium approached, Moore created *Tom Strong*, a superman character that takes the concept back to basics by invoking the pulp and legendary archetypes that inspired Superman. Moore tells these stories with a simple, primal appeal.

One of Moore's favourite story devices has been to take superheroes out of their storybook world and place them in a world more like our own. Moore wasn't the first person to try to treat superheroes realistically, or to imagine them operating in the real world. From the late sixties on, a number of titles reflected social changes and fears. *The X-Men* portrayed a group of people feared by society at large, and the arguments between the peaceable Professor X and the militant Magneto echoed those between Martin Luther King and Malcolm X. A celebrated run of *Green Lantern/ Green Arrow* by Denny O'Neil and artist Neal Adams had dealt with issues of racism, poverty and drug abuse. Poor black city dwellers berated Green Lantern for worrying more about alien invasions than "real problems." Green Arrow's kid partner, Speedy, became a heroin addict.

The seventies saw a new generation of socially aware superheroes like Hawk and Dove – one a soldier, the other a pacifist – and superheroes who could never be allowed to forget their ethnic origin, like Black Lightning and Black Panther. Some of these were clever, well-told tales. Others were simply embarrassing. The worst was almost certainly *Lois Lane* 106, in which (thanks to Kryptonian technology) she became a black woman for a day to research a story. All of them – good or bad – reflected the fact that publishers were beginning to recognise that comics were being read by an older, more sophisticated audience than had traditionally been the case.

Outside comics, other authors addressed the problems inherent in superheroes. Larry Niven's widely reprinted 1971 essay 'Man Of Steel, Woman Of Kleenex' speculated about Superman's sex life and the practicalities of being invulnerable and super-strong. One big influence on Moore seems to have been the satirical novel *Super-Folks* by Robert Mayer (1977), about a Superman-like hero who has retired, grown fat and become increasingly impotent in any number of ways. Moore's work echoes the book in a number of places: the idea of Superman giving it all up to live a normal life has been a recurring theme; the police going on strike because the superheroes are stealing their jobs is a key plot point in *Watchmen*; also, *Super-Folks* and 'Whatever Happened To The Man Of Tomorrow?' have the same ending – a formerly mischievous but now truly evil pixie character is behind the events of both. Moore has said that *Super-Folks* was "a big influence on *Marvelman*. By the time I did the last Superman stories I'd forgotten the Mayer book, although I may have had it subconsciously in my mind, but it was certainly influential on *Marvelman* and the idea of placing superheroes in hard times and in a browbeaten real world."

But Moore's approach went beyond espousing liberal causes or pointing out the logical shortcomings of superhero comics. At the end of the eighties, Moore and a precious few others seemed about to initiate a shift that would see the comic book – sequential art, or whatever you want to call it – become an accepted medium, as it is in France, Italy and Japan. It would be as easy and as socially acceptable to buy a comic as a book or a CD. Moore was the most prominent figurehead of the revolution in comics that had hit the industry in the late eighties. For a few years, comics boomed – sales and back issue prices rocketed, publishers found themselves signing six-figure royalty cheques, and the promised land of mainstream acceptability seemed only a few steps away. Comic books were rebranded as graphic novels, and their writers were invited onto literary review programmes and treated like any other novelist. Long articles in colour supplements discussed the iconic stature of Superman and the significance of Batman. Avid fans, new readers and the literary establishment alike lapped comics up.

Alan Moore was at the centre of this revolution. Indeed, in James Park's 1991 book, *Cultural Icons*, his entry is longer than Madonna's or Robert de Niro's, and only a couple of lines shorter than the entry for The Beatles. Along with *Dark Knight Returns*, Moore's *Watchmen* was the book that everyone who was anyone was reading. It invaded pop culture in a way that seems barely plausible now – Bomb the Bass adopted the

Watchmen badge (a smiley face with a splash of blood) as its own, and it became one of the great images of 1987. Terry Gilliam was going to direct the film. It was possible to buy a leather-bound slipcase edition of the story. The summer of 1989 saw Tim Burton's *Batman* break box-office records. While most contemporary publicity suggested that Burton's film was an adaptation of *Dark Knight Returns*, it actually bears little resemblance to Miller's story – the retro-Forties look and the Batman/Joker relationship came from Moore's *The Killing Joke*. That year, the chorus of *Can U Dig It* by Pop Will Eat Itself proclaimed "Alan Moore knows the score."

The obvious question to ask, then, is "where did it all go wrong?"

Ten years on, most large bookshops still have a small graphic novel section, and films like *Unbreakable* and *The Matrix* are steeped in the comic book sensibility, but it seems like an awfully long time since Penguin Books published graphic novels. After a few years, comics retreated to their comic shop ghettos. Despite all the promises of cataclysmic changes in the way the comic industry is run, ten years later the meat and drink of the comic book industry is still stories about musclemen and pneumatic women punching each other. The fact that cinema can get the masses to watch superheroes like Batman, Spider-Man and the X-Men only makes comics' failure to capture the imagination more depressing.

As the Nineties began, the economy turned from boom to bust and the value of people's comics collections collapsed like the price of houses, vintage cars and Impressionist paintings. There was also increased competition for young men's money – computer games, sell-through videos and more magazines targeted at them. But even so, comics are relatively cheap items, and should have weathered the storm.

Quite simply the boom ended because there weren't enough good comics out there to appeal to people. If you want to watch great cinema, you can watch a classic film a week and you'll die before you've seen them all. Likewise with classic novels, music, even television programmes – you're spoiled for choice. In a recent guide to writing comics in *Wizard* magazine, industry stalwart Mark Waid stated that the only comics you actually need to read are *Watchmen*, *Maus* and *Dark Knight Returns*, all of which were written in the eighties. Even with an expanded list, if you want to read all the great comics, you really don't need to take more than a week off work. The people who came to the medium because of *Watchmen* quickly left – there was little more to see. DC's Vertigo imprint remains, but it's often been little more than a pale shadow of Moore. *Swamp Thing* continued without him, various members of the supporting cast appeared in other series. John Constantine, created by Moore for *Swamp Thing*, has appeared for fifteen years in his own contemporary horror title, *Hellblazer*. *The Sandman*, one of the few successful comic books to appeal to non-comics fans, was often, in its early days, little more than a replay of a few of Moore's *Swamp Thing* riffs. Those are among the best. Far too many of Moore's imitators took realism to mean an adolescent preoccupation with bodily fluids and swear words. None of Moore's intricate, thoughtful use of the medium, let alone his sense of humour and playfulness, survives. And as for superheroes... when the bubble burst, comics companies played it safe. They couldn't afford to support loss-leader product, so they desperately tried to retain a collectors' market by issuing superficialities like variant covers and gimmicky stories.

Alan Moore was, again, a crucial figure. A prolific, high-profile writer, Moore severed his ties with DC in the late eighties, set up his own company, Mad Love, and started doing more avant-garde work for independent publishers. It was an exciting prospect – the equivalent of Spielberg breaking away from the studio system and setting up DreamWorks SKG. But the recession turned a sure thing into disaster – even the major companies hit serious trouble, and Marvel, the biggest publisher in the industry, filed for bankruptcy in 1997. Mad Love collapsed. Moore's projects became dogged with production and distribution problems.

From Hell is the best case in point. It is an extraordinary piece of work, easily in the *Watchmen/Dark Knight Returns/Maus* league. Taking on the Jack the Ripper legend, Moore created a postmodernist masterpiece – a comprehensively-researched analysis of the case, which doesn't shy away from a visceral depiction of violent acts, but imbues them with symbolic and metaphorical importance. Moore and artist Eddie Campbell have created a world where contemporary engraving and portraits come to scratchy life. At first, it couldn't be further from the glossy, colourful worlds of *Watchmen* or *The Killing Joke*, but the style becomes compelling, integral to the story being told. This isn't simply a prose novel with pictures, or the storyboards for a film – it has to be a comic strip. At heart, it's a great story, an utterly compelling solution to the murders that then deconstructs itself. It moves the comic strip form forward.

But, almost from the start, *From Hell* was plagued with difficulties. Moore started work on the series in 1988, but it would be ten years before the last instalment was published. Originally intended to appear in Steve Bissette's horror anthology *Taboo*, and then collected into comic book format, the series was hit twice, first by the collapse of *Taboo* and then the bankruptcy of Tundra. Even switching publishers, *From Hell* appeared irregularly – no more than two issues a year, seemingly released at random intervals. Distribution was patchy – it was a resolutely uncommercial prospect, with each issue being black and white and having a high cover price, and comic retailers were in the middle of a distribution crisis. Customs and police seized the consignments in a number of countries including Australia, South Africa and England. Collecting the entire series was beyond the abilities of even some of Moore's most dedicated fans, and all critical or sales momentum was lost.

Now, ironically, it could become Moore's best-known work, as it has been made into a film starring Johnny Depp and Heather Graham. *From Hell* is utterly unfilmable – it's a vast work, full of digressions and subplots. Ironically, the film feels exactly like the sort of lurid horror comic that *From Hell* isn't. With its chirpy working-class hero kicking against the establishment, drug-induced visions and a sprinkling of mild nudity it's a sub-Moore Vertigo comic brought to life. As with other postmodern books that become films, like *The English Patient*, the ambiguities and multilayered storytelling have been stripped away in favour of a whodunnit and love story. The film alternates between frame by frame loyalty to the original graphic novel and wholesale abandoning of its historical accuracy and story logic. Shifting the story from a psychological investigation of Jack the Ripper to a conventional whodunnit causes all sorts of problems with the plotting and pacing, and sometimes the effects of the changes just haven't been thought through – Abberline knows Mary Kelly and her friends in the film, he knows that the Ripper is offering his victims drugged grapes... but never thinks to tell the prostitutes what to look out for. The film surprised many film pundits by going to number one at the US Box Office the week of release, but it's an above-average thriller, nothing more than that. Whatever the case, the original comics have now been collected into a trade paperback, and the film will concentrate critical attention on the story for the first time.

In the mid-nineties, Moore returned to superhero comics. No doubt he could have made a very comfortable living ploughing the same furrows he had in the eighties, or won awards for more avant-garde work, but Moore had no interest in that. Instead he horrified some of his fans by writing colourful superhero books. Moore created a revolution, then disowned it. He renounced the crass commercialism of superheroes, then returned to write for Image comics, surely the most crassly commercial publisher he could have hoped to find. After a period while he concentrated on other long-held interests like performance art and magic shows which now drew greater attention because of his raised profile, he has returned to create a range of colourful, archetypal comics characters. And his work is as fresh and innovative as it's ever been. In a market that's struggling, both *2000AD* and Marvel recognise that to sign him would help reverse their ailing fortunes. After more than two decades in the toils, Alan Moore remains a central creative force in comics, and their best hope.

2. The British Years

Secret Origins

Alan Moore started, as most British comics writers have, by graduating from drawing for local magazines to writing one-off strips for a variety of magazines, gradually building a reputation and being allowed to tell the sort of stories he wanted to, rather than ones dictated by a limited page count and the needs of an editor. As with every freelancer, at first Moore had to identify magazines that would pay money to comic strip writers, and work to their strictures.

Moore began contributing to xeroxed Northampton Arts Lab magazines, *Embryo* and *Rovel*. His work at the time was clearly influenced by magazines like *Oz*, and included poems, comic strips, art and prose. A picture used as an advertisement for the SF shop Dark They Were And Golden Eyed in 1969 in the pages of the British underground comic *Cyclops* marked his first appearance in anything approaching a professional magazine.

After being expelled from school at seventeen for dealing acid, he had a succession of menial jobs, such as working in a sheep-skinning yard and cleaning toilets at the Grand Hotel in Northampton. During the seventies, Moore came close to a breakthrough a couple of times, as a number of publishers and editors toyed with new superhero or SF comics, but these all fell through – until the success of the movies *Star Wars* and *Superman*, publishers doubted there would be a large audience for science fiction, fantasy or superheroes. An early sample sent to DC Thomson was set in a fascist future and involved a costumed character known as The Doll, concepts which later resurfaced in *V for Vendetta* but was unsuitable for Thomson's young audience. Undaunted, Moore – then working in an office and with a baby on the way – continued to explore opportunities to create illustrations and comic strips.

'Anon E. Mouse' was produced for the local underground paper *Anon*, followed by 'St. Pancras Panda' – which Moore describes as "Paddington Bear in Hell" – for *Back Street Bugle*, an Oxford-based alternative magazine, which was Moore's first experience of meeting deadlines, and creating punchlines for the fortnightly episodes. For *Dark Star*, a fanzine for west coast music, Moore worked with Steve Moore (no relation), whom he had known since the age of 14, on 'Three Eyes McGurk And His Death Planet Commandos' which featured the first appearance (and subsequent death) of Axel Pressbutton. The strip, pencilled by Moore, was picked up by Gilbert Shelton for the British New Talent issue of the American underground *Rip-Off Comix*.

His first professional sale – as none of his work to date had been paid – were illustrations to the music magazine *NME*. Realising that illustrations alone would not support him, Moore submitted a strip to *Sounds* which began to appear (as by Curt Vile) in early 1979: 'Roscoe Moscow' was a satirical strip encompassing music, nuclear war, fascism and aliens, which Moore followed up with 'The Stars My Degradation,' with Steve Moore, which combined *Star Wars* imagery with the playful subversion of underground comix. His second regular paying gig – ten pounds a week – was 'Maxwell The Magic Cat,' which he wrote and drew for his local newspaper, the *Northants Post*. The strip started in 1979, and Moore continued to supply a strip each and every week until 1986 – well beyond the point he was making good money from his American work. Maxwell seemed conceived as an antidote to Garfield and, instead of ending with a twee joke or trite homily, tended to dwell on the everyday – strikes and riots or, more often, that cats ate mice and had fleas. While some of the strips are funny and imaginative, it would be a stretch to say that *Maxwell* was great, but it remains easily Moore's longest running continuing series and the strips are interesting snapshots of how his mind works.

1980 represented a turning point, as Moore started working for the weekly *2000AD*, published by IPC. The comic had only been around since 1977, but was selling well, and had become an important focus for the British comics scene – and one character in particular, Judge Dredd, had quickly become very popular. The production values on *2000AD* were primitive by current standards. As with every other British comic of the time, it was printed on newsprint, and expensive colour pages were reserved for the centre spread and the cover (so limited was the use of colour that half the artists working on early Judge Dredd strips thought he was black, the other half thought he was white!). Each issue had five or six strips, around four to eight pages each. Only Judge Dredd appeared every week without fail, and there was a balance between other established, long-running series like The A.B.C. Warriors and Strontium Dog and one-off stories, often only two or three pages, with a simple twist or shock ending – although the banners they usually appeared under, 'Tharg's Future Shocks' and 'Ro-Jaws' Robo-Tales' blunted the sting a little. One seemingly minor innovation was having huge consequences – the artist and writer were credited for their work and comics were suddenly something that people wrote, not things that magically appeared. If you were interested, you could follow the work of your favourite writers and artists as easily as you could the characters, and this led to *2000AD*'s readers becoming ever more literate in the medium. In the book *Writers On Comics Scriptwriting*, acclaimed writers Garth Ennis and Warren Ellis both trace their interest in writing comics to one article in the 1981 *2000AD* annual (which, as is traditional with British annuals trying to prolong their shelf life, actually came out in the autumn of the year before the cover date). The annual printed a *Judge Dredd* script and explained how it was made into a comic strip.

Moore's earliest published work for *2000AD* appeared around the same time as the 1981 Annual – his very first was 'A Holiday In Hell' in the 1980 *Sci-Fi Special*, and he would provide the comic with one or two of these every month for the next few years. With only two or three pages to work with, and without always knowing who would draw the strip, Moore had little room for manoeuvre. Everyone writing the one-off strips relied on a simple formula – weak puns, black humour and someone dying horribly at the end through their misadventures. Moore could hack the pace easily enough. One early strip, 'The Dating Game' is a case in point. It's notable now for being the first collaboration between Moore and his *Watchmen* co-creator Dave Gibbons. The story is about a man living in the near future who fills in a computer dating form and … can you guess? … ends up dating a computer. The story then turns to *Fatal Attraction* territory, with the man pursued relentlessly across the city by the spurned computer, which controls various electronic devices. The man dies horribly when he's pulled into a robot litter bin.

Some of Moore's later *2000AD* one-off strips are minor masterpieces. 'Sunburn' is set in a holiday camp built on a sunspot, a wonderfully surreal creation, with Pallor Parlours full of people trying to lose their suntan, and where the policemen are called Suntries. Although he had no control over the artists chosen to draw his strips, he was teamed up with some of *2000AD*'s leading names. Jesus Redondo provided some truly eerie visuals to atmospheric stories like 'Ring Road' and 'The Time Machine.' Moore and Dave Gibbons told some intricate and absurd tales like 'The Disturbed Digestions Of Doctor Dibworthy' and 'Chronocops,' the last of which is a tour-de-force comic story in which a couple of *Dragnet*-inspired hardboiled policemen ("My name's Saturday. Joe Saturday. I'm a cop. I like my coffee weak and sugary. I like my women the same. I speak in short sentences. I'm just a guy, doing his job") try to protect history from time-travelling criminals intent on killing their own grandparents and causing temporal paradoxes. Moore clearly still has affection for the form – many of the *Tomorrow Stories* that he writes for ABC nowadays would not be out of place as *Future Shocks* or *Time Twisters* – the *Jack B Quick* strip in particular is a descendant of a number of "too clever by half" characters like Abelard Snazz.

There were a number of British magazines looking for work like this – Moore contributed a couple of similar strips to the new *Eagle*, *Doctor Who Weekly* and *Scream!* as well as filler text stories for a variety of magazines and annuals. It would seem to be a fairly thankless task, but as a generation of British writers and artists were discovering, this was a remarkably good apprenticeship. It meant that a writer could see how different artists interpreted scripts, made a number of contacts in the comics' scene, learned what was popular with audiences and what editors were looking for. In terms of storytelling, it imposed an economy and efficiency to the narrative and forced writers to come up with imaginative solutions and striking images and ideas. Moore's technique quickly developed in this environment.

His work for Marvel UK's *Doctor Who* is a case in point. It starts with a back-up strip 'Black Legacy' featuring the Cybermen facing a mystery secret weapon – there are a couple of poignant moments, but little to distinguish it from the work being done by his namesake Steve Moore, the regular writer. His second story featured the Autons, monsters that had made two appearances in the TV show in the early seventies. 'Business As Usual' has a strong narrative and a few striking images, but is essentially a rerun of the televised Auton stories. But Moore is clearly more confident and his next story, a depiction of the early days of the Time Lords of Gallifrey, is an early, if minor, landmark. The history of the Doctor's people has always been shrouded in mystery and contradiction in the TV series – one story says the founder of the Time Lords was the "solar engineer" Omega, in subsequent tales that honour falls to the political leader Rassilon. Moore resolves the contradiction by making them contemporaries – a solution only later adopted by the TV series itself. More importantly, the strip allows Moore an almost free reign – he seems to be deliberately steering the narrative clear of what we might expect to see, based on the 'facts' established on television: Omega is never seen, Rassilon is only glimpsed, there are no attempts to tie the visuals of the strip to the appearances of Gallifrey in the TV series. Instead, Moore creates his own characters, including the enigmatic Black Sun, all but unseen, who are destined to fight a war with the Time Lords in the future. Moore's work here and elsewhere was an influence on the later production teams of the Sylvester McCoy period (Moore would decline the chance to write for the 1988 season), and these three simple back-up strips have continued as an influence on several of the *Doctor Who* novels that succeeded the TV series in the nineties.

Captain Britain

Working with Marvel UK led to Moore's first regular series, and the first opportunity for him to make his presence known. Thanks largely to the success of *2000AD*, the British comics scene was cohering as never before, and it was clear that the audience was sticking with the title as they grew up. Comics were no longer just for very small boys: teenagers – even A-Level and university students – were reading them now. Marvel UK had traditionally been a limited operation which did little more than repackage American superhero material for a British audience that had never really understood the appeal of superheroes. But the staff was growing and titles like *Star Wars* and *Doctor Who* were printing original material. In the early eighties, Marvel started to print titles for the slightly older, more sophisticated, market that *2000AD* had discovered. Along with reprints of material like Frank Miller's run on *Daredevil*, there was room for new material, primarily the home-grown superhero Captain Britain. Moore took over the strip from writer Dave Thorpe and inherited the series' artist, Alan Davis. Davis had debuted professionally only a few months earlier but, by the time Moore was writing, he'd developed into a strong, distinctive draftsman (nowadays he's a stalwart of the American comics scene). It was a partnership that worked, and they would collaborate on a number of other projects.

Captain Britain under Dave Thorpe was a weird mix of science fiction thriller, high fantasy, political allegory and contemporary drama as Thorpe tried to drag the strip away from its roots (it was originally created, written and drawn in America for the British audience). Moore immediately asserted his own authority on the strip, killing Jackdaw, Captain Britain's elfish companion, in his first instalment, obliterating Captain Britain himself in the second so he had to be recreated from scratch, and eventually blowing up the whole universe Thorpe had set his stories in. Moore also shipped in the Special Executive from his *Doctor Who Monthly* strips, and he and Davis would later sneak in a few Marvelman cameos. Despite that, Moore never quite got away from the earlier encumbrances, and the story ends with an acknowledged reprise of Thorpe's last story, with the "crooked man" Jim Jaspers gaining power and trying to wipe out all superheroes. There are some great sequences and the Fury, a relentless biomechanical assassin that pursues Captain Britain across universes, is a memorable creation, but despite a consistency in the art and a huge amount of imagination, the strip never quite coheres.

Moore's extra-curricular work for *The Daredevils* is arguably just as significant. Although these text pieces grew out of the simple problem of trying to stretch a small budget, Moore and others used the opportunity to create a forum to air their views about the genre, to help give voice to the new, older comics fans. Moore wrote an appreciation of Frank Miller, a slightly less appreciative article about Marvel publisher Stan Lee (such criticism had been unheard of in a Marvel title before), articles about sexism in comics and even a fanzine review column. Along with photos of creators and comic conventions, circumstance dictated that *The Daredevils* became an unconscious attempt to solidify the British comic audience, with Moore as one of its point men.

Warrior

Although his work for Marvel and in *2000AD* gave Moore a high profile with the younger British comics audience, it would be at another company that Moore would start to reach his potential. Dez Skinn, drawing on his experiences as an editor at both IPC and Marvel UK, was putting together a new monthly magazine to appeal to older readers, *Warrior*. Most important, it would offer creators a degree of freedom unheard of at Marvel or IPC. Skinn wanted to revive the fifties British superhero Marvelman, and had read an interview with Moore in which the writer had said he wished someone would bring the character back so he could write for the series. Moore, Skinn and artist David Lloyd also agreed Moore would write another cornerstone title, the political thriller *V For Vendetta*. Moore would also contribute a couple of spin-off strips from *Marvelman*, and the comedy *The Bojeffries Saga*.

Marvelman and *V For Vendetta* debuted in the launch issue of *Warrior* (March 1982), and introduced themes which would recur throughout his work; both showed what Moore was capable of given the freedom and space to develop his stories.

V For Vendetta

V For Vendetta is set in (the then distant) 1997, in a Britain ruled by fascists who have taken power after a limited nuclear war, and the resulting environmental disaster has led to society's collapse. Led by the puritanical Adam Susan, the fascists have rounded up and killed everyone they consider to be a subversive – blacks, gays, radicals – leaving a docile, scared populace. Into this arrives V, a man hidden behind a Guy Fawkes mask, an anarchist and terrorist who is, it seems, enacting a very elaborate and specific revenge on the fascist leadership. His campaign starts with the destruction of the Houses of Parliament, and the story is split pretty evenly between the police investigation into his actions and the depiction of V's next act. In the first chapter, V rescues a sixteen-year-old girl, Evey Hammond, and begins to involve her in his schemes. She finds it difficult to stomach the violent methods V uses, but discovers that the world is an even more dangerous and violent place when she loses V's protection.

V For Vendetta represents a perfect match between subject and artwork – David Lloyd's regular panels are full of what often seem like optical illusions, or abstract patterns, but they resolve into people and buildings. Everything is presented in stark black or white, the panels are carefully composed, often mirroring or juxtaposed against each other. It's a confident technique, and it's no surprise to learn that Moore and Lloyd were in constant communication with each other, and playing to each other's strengths. Moore is notorious for providing detailed scripts – while some of his colleagues can describe a whole page in a couple of sentences, Moore can take a couple of pages of script to describe a single panel. In his earlier work, this attention to detail isn't always obvious from the final result – but it's all too easy to imagine that the scripts for *V For Vendetta* were particularly elaborate.

V For Vendetta is still among Moore's best work; it works as a detective story, a futuristic thriller, an action adventure, a depiction of an ideological struggle. V's actions are unsettling, his methods appalling. While the fascists have homes and families, V is faceless, remorseless. There is a clash of ideologies, but V's brand of enforced anarchy seems just as dictatorial as fascism. Ordinary people are caught in the middle of this. But if they are victims, the suggestion is they have made their own cage – people can be ruled or not, there's no middle ground.

Unsurprisingly, *V* gained a lot of attention and a cult following. David J from the group Bauhaus collaborated with Moore to write the song *This Vicious Cabaret*. There was a student film which Moore and Lloyd provided help with. The series won a number of Eagle Awards, set up to celebrate excellence in British comics, and even got mentioned in Time Out.

The publication of *V For Vendetta* was suspended when *Warrior* folded, inadvertently creating one of the greatest cliffhangers in comics –

one lost now halfway through issue seven of the DC reprints, or page 166 of the trade paperback. It would be four years before the end of the story was told. When the *Warrior* material was reprinted by DC in American comic book form it was colourised, which ought to have ruined it, but the work was carefully supervised by Lloyd, and the palette is one of washed-out pastel colours; the result is as haunting as the original.

Marvelman

Marvelman is a character that came with a convoluted and litigious publishing history which continues to dog the character to the present day. In the Forties the popularity of the DC character Superman, the first 'superhero,' led to a lot of imitators. One in particular, Captain Marvel, was particularly popular, outselling *Superman* most months – and for good reason: the publishers, Fawcett, used experienced illustrators, whereas DC tended to use artists fresh from high school. DC sued, saying Captain Marvel was almost identical to their character, but lost on a technicality. The legal battle continued for over ten years. In 1953, with superhero comics on the wane, Fawcett agreed to stop publishing *Captain Marvel* (a few years later, ironically, DC would acquire the rights to publish the character). *Captain Marvel* was reprinted in Britain, and was very popular – the publishers Miller and Sons were loathe to end the series, but ran out of material. Instead they made a few superficial changes and the character metamorphosed into *Marvelman* in 1954. That strip ended in 1963.

Moore's concept for *Marvelman* was simple – he took a kitsch children's character and placed him within the real world of 1982. The Fifties character had inhabited a bright, pre-Lapsarian world, where people were optimistic atomic power would solve all the world's problems (the magic word "Kimota" that gave Marvelman his power was "atomic" backwards) and everything was carefree and timeless. Moore's story starts with the threat of terrorism at a nuclear power plant, and the opening chapters take pains to place events firmly in the ordinary, contemporary, world with references to everything from the Brixton riots to Adam And The Ants.

Middle-aged Mike Moran rediscovers his magic word accidentally, and saying it he transforms into the absurdly powerful Marvelman, invulnerable, super-strong, able to fly. As he does, his memories begin to return. The story takes the basic thrill of superhero comics for the reader – imagining having such great powers – and begins to explore the implications. At first it means exhilaration – the pleasure of flight and demonstrations of strength, even down to acknowledging that owning a beyond-perfect body would have benefits for your sex life. But as this is the real world, the negative side to this new-found power becomes obvious. There are vested interests keen to curb Marvelman's power – it becomes clear that the government were involved in both Marvelman's creation and his subsequent amnesia and disappearance. Marvelman's one-time sidekick, Kid Marvelman, never lost his memories and has spent years building a powerful business empire and nurturing his resentment of Marvelman. He's evil, with all Marvelman's powers and twenty years more experience.

Moore has a lot of fun playing against the expectations of superhero comics. In one scene, Liz buys a pile of comics to run up a checklist of Marvelman's powers. In a later instalment, it's revealed that the mad scientist who created Marvelman, Gargunza, was inspired by a *Captain Marvel* comic (a British reprint!) discarded in the works canteen. But the key difference between *Marvelman* and ordinary superhero comics is that things change. Instead of the endless unrequited Lois and Superman relationship, Marvelman and Liz sleep together, have a child, and Liz leaves home when she can't cope with the way her life has changed. Heroes kill, to prevent further deaths, but their enemies are utterly ruthless – kidnapping and murdering supporting players, or destroying London just to draw attention to themselves.

Marvelman And V In America

Moore was given a lot of leeway in *Warrior* and was allowed, for the first time, to tackle longer stories and more adult themes – for a short time at least. *Warrior* would only run for twenty-six issues, and a number of problems, including legal disputes, prevented *Marvelman* from appearing in the last five of those. This means that both *Marvelman* and *V* were left unfinished for several years. Once Moore was working in America, both series were picked up and Moore was able to complete them (with Marvelman renamed Miracleman following objections from Marvel Comics).

It is interesting to note that Moore conceived both series as finite stories with a beginning, middle and end in mind as the opening chapters unfolded. Most comic strips at the time were designed to play out endlessly, and had *Warrior* continued, it's entirely possible that younger fans imagined *V For Vendetta* running endlessly, with V blowing up a new symbol of fascist rule every month, just as *Judge Dredd* has replayed a few simple riffs over a thousand times in *2000AD*. Unlike the early *2000AD* strip *Invasion* (in which the Volgans, thinly-disguised Russians who invaded the United Kingdom in the 1990s, faced the challenge of the resistance leader Bill Savage, who attacked them every week with no apparent long-term strategy), V has a plan – which we are not privy to. By the end of Book One his 'vendetta' is looking more and more like an elaborate cover story: he's no longer destroying individuals that persecuted him at the Larkhill Resettlement Camp, and his vengeance broadens first to attacking the state, then to attacking the very notion of states. As early as spring 1984, Moore was saying (in an interview in issue 10 of the fanzine *Arkensword*) that "there is a basic unwinding of the mystery throughout the three volumes that make up the V trilogy, and there hopefully will be a satisfying revelation at the end."

With *Marvelman*, the foreshadowing was more clear cut: as early as issue 4's story 'The Yesterday Gambit,' we are told that 1985 will see an apocalyptic battle between the hero and his arch-enemy. This came to pass in Book Three, as Kid Miracleman destroys London in issue 15 of the American title (and, had *Warrior* continued and the same material appeared in eight-page chapters every month, that battle would indeed have been published in late 1985). There are a few minor changes (Big Ben changes his name to avoid a copyright dispute and The Silence, Marvelman's base in the flash-forward, is little more than an afterthought in the final strip), but there are early signs Moore had a limited run in mind. When Marvelman confronts his arch-enemy Emil Gargunza in Book Two, Gargunza is killed, he's not given a chance to escape to fight again à la Lex Luthor or the Joker, as he might have been in a running series. At the same time, *Miracleman* did continue, once Moore left the title, with Neil Gaiman fully intending to write three books of his own, until the publisher Eclipse hit financial problems.

Miracleman did not have a happy history in the States – early issues sold well, but the original *Warrior* pages were horribly recoloured, and reduced from their intended size. When Alan Davis' material ran out, Chuck Beckum did not prove an adequate replacement, and Rick Veitch's work, while an improvement, was for some reason not up to the standards he'd set for himself over on Moore's *Swamp Thing*. Book Three's artist, John Totleben, was a marked improvement ... but the book didn't maintain any sort of regular schedule, which in turn started to affect the distribution and sales of the comic. That all seems irrelevant now – *Miracleman* completed its run, and Book Three is a fine piece of work, as epic and intricate a statement on the superhero genre as *Watchmen*, but without sacrificing any of the action or energy for the sake of form or structure. As it happened, *Marvelman/Miracleman*'s legal problems were just beginning: Eclipse would go bankrupt in the early 1990s, and a variety of people would end up claiming they had the rights to, variously, the character, the original artwork and the right to reprint. It's a situation that has kept Moore's story out of print for ten years, making it one of his most sought-after works for collectors. In a characteristically ironic twist, Marvel Comics, the company that threatened to sue *Warrior* and forced the change of name, received much press in 2001 when Editor-In-Chief Joe Quesada said that they would be willing to republish the series under its original title, although turning that desire into a reality still depends very much on an ongoing battle over copyrights.

V For Vendetta had no such problems – the series was completed by the original artist, David Lloyd, to a regular schedule. It was promptly collected as a trade paperback, and is in print today.

As originally presented, *Marvelman* and *V For Vendetta* ran alongside each other in *Warrior*, and both stories unfold over three "Books" of roughly equal length. Had *Warrior* continued, both stories would have concluded around issue 40. Reading them together throws up some interesting contrasts – in one the hero fights a fascist dictatorship based in London, in the other an Aryan superman imposes one.

One of Moore's favourite techniques, one he's singled out as a great advantage of the comics medium, is juxtaposition. Comics mix words and pictures – and it's common in Moore's work to be presented with a caption and picture that seem rather incongruous. Often this creates a simple ironic effect (as at the end of *The Killing Joke*, where one of Batman's lines from the beginning of the story "Hello, I came to talk" reappears above a picture of Batman poised to attack the Joker), but sometimes there is a more thoughtful, poetic effect, as in *A Small Killing*, where the captions show Timothy Hole musing about the exact order of his collection of birds' eggs as the pictures show him involved in a serious car crash. Reading *Warrior*, there is the sense that *Marvelman* and *V For Vendetta* are being deliberately contrasted. *V* has a dark look to it, full of regular, perfectly composed frames. *Marvelman* is far more fluid and, particularly when Alan Davis draws it, almost cartoony. *V* is set at street level, in the everyday world of houses and offices. *Marvelman* soon transcends that, taking in exotic locales – secret government bunkers, jungles, even the inside of an alien spacecraft.

But despite that, there are plenty of points of correspondence: the authorities trying and utterly failing to track down, control, or even to understand, the hero; the fragility of the symbols of society, and by extension society itself – both see the Houses of Parliament destroyed as the prelude to a new era (it happens at the start of *V* and near the conclusion of *Marvelman*). The stories run at roughly the same pace: in the first book, the hero is revealed in a public demonstration of his power, which alerts the police and their political masters to his presence. As the authorities close in on the hero, it becomes clear that the hero is the result of an experiment the government had conducted years ago, a dark secret they thought was buried, but which now threatens to destroy them. The most interesting parallel is that the everyman character in both is a woman – Liz Moran, Marvelman's wife, and Evey Hammond, a teenage girl rescued by V from a life, or quick death, in prostitution and taken under his wing. Both are used by Moore to represent normal, honest, human morality, and to contrast that with the hero's amorality – V's beliefs mean he has no compunction about murder, and, for Marvelman too, the constraints and rules of human society seem increasingly irrelevant; as one character says, from his perspective, man is little more than an animal. Both Liz and Evey argue with their heroes, attempt to challenge their certainties. And both Liz and Evey are cast out (Liz marginalised, Evey simply ejected), unable to cope and left searching for a normal life. Evey is drawn back in, eventually taking V's mask and continuing his work. But when Marvelman finds Liz, she refuses the treatment that would make her into a superhuman.

While both are impressive pieces of work on their own, reading them together it becomes clear that Moore is exploring wider notions of "normality" and the British way of life. Both Marvelman and V are individuals capable of bringing down a whole society. Both are a challenge to the things we take for granted. In both the forces of law and order have vested interests, intent on preserving their own power at any cost, but who, through their own selfish, sadistic actions, cause the hero to be created. *V* is dystopian, *Marvelman* is, or at least ends, on a utopian note, but by running both strips at the same time, in the same magazine, Moore seems to be asking us to question any notion of an easy, imposed solution for mankind's problems. Fascist Britain is a utopia, or promises to be, for those in charge of it – one man's perfect world is not necessarily anyone else's. *Marvelman* also invites comparison with Moore's *Captain Britain* work (especially as they end up with the same artist). Telling stories in the Marvel universe, Moore distances *Captain Britain* from the "realism" of *Marvelman*, revelling in the parallel universes and aliens that would shatter the central conceit of his *Warrior* work.

Within a few years, Moore's strategy with *Marvelman* would start a revolution in comics. His formula was used by other writers to revamp dozens upon dozens of superheroes, from the completely obscure (*Animal*

Man, The Sandman, Shade The Changing Man) to the bedrock characters of the genre like Superman, Batman and Wonder Woman. Nearly twenty years on, both the first issue of *The Sentry* (Marvel Comics, 2000) and the film *Unbreakable* (2000, written and directed by M Knight Shyamalan) use exactly the same story as *Marvelman*: a married, middle-aged man discovers that he is Superman.

While *V* is perhaps the more sophisticated, overtly political work, the market for comics was (as it still is) dominated by superhero stories. So it was Moore's work on *Marvelman* that caught the attention of the big American publishers. Moore had become disenchanted with Marvel, feeling both he and others had been badly treated, and didn't want to work for them any more (a sentiment he continues to reiterate). So it was that he was snapped up by Marvel's great rival, DC Comics, to become the new regular writer on *Swamp Thing*.

The Bojeffries Saga

Moore's third regular strip for *Warrior* was the often overlooked *The Bojeffries Saga*, which follows the lives of the Bojeffries, who manage to resemble both the Addams and Royle families. It's a slice of working-class life, with a working family of werewolves, vampires and other grotesques. Moore's gift for comedy is often ignored. His ability to use the comic strip to give his characters perfect comic timing, to set up elaborate running verbal and visual jokes, to expose ironies and to populate panels with hilarious incidental details is a key part of his appeal. That said, the main meat of *The Bojeffries Saga* is the details of everyday life, slightly exaggerated. 'Raoul's Night Out' is the best example of this. It follows Raoul, the poodle-eating werewolf member of the family, as he goes to work, then for a night out with his colleagues.

Hanging Out With Halo Jones, D.R. And Quinch

As *Warrior* started to hit problems, Moore was starting to break into the American market. The *Marvelman* strip vanished after issue 21 (August 1984), and *Warrior* itself wouldn't last much longer (the final issue appeared in February 1985), dooming a planned collaboration with Bryan Talbot, *Nightjar*, to oblivion. At the same time, Moore was cutting his ties with Marvel UK, with his last *Captain Britain* strip appearing in

June 1984. The only significant British publication left for Moore was *2000AD*.

In the past, Moore had supplied *2000AD* with a great number of filler and one-off strips, but those days were past – his last such story (barring one for an Annual and a rather backhanded one-page return in issue 500) appeared in August 1983. In 1982, he had been invited to write a longer serial, *Skizz*, inspired by the early buzz for an upcoming Steven Spielberg movie, *E.T.: The Extraterrestrial*. From this brief, Moore created a charming strip about a little alien who crash-landed in Birmingham. Skizz was an alien interpreter, told by the computer of his crashed spaceship that he'd need all his advanced technology to survive on such a savage planet … and that the craft was just about to self-destruct, as it was illegal under galactic law to bring advanced technology to such a savage planet. Skizz survived thanks to a teenaged girl, Roxy, and her friends, who managed to rescue Skizz from the clutches of the evil South African Mr Van Owen. It's a funny strip, and you really end up caring about the characters, but despite Moore's attempts to subvert the brief he had been given by giving the strip a realistic setting, its thunder was comprehensively stolen by *E.T.*, which appeared in the cinemas some months earlier; later *Skizz* instalments even had the characters commenting on the similarities.

In 1984 Moore created two strips which are fondly remembered by *2000AD* readers, despite being relatively short-lived. The first, which had grown from one of his *Time Twisters* one-off stories, was 'D.R. & Quinch Have Fun On Earth,' drawn by his *Marvelman* and *Captain Britain* collaborator, Alan Davis. These appeared in early 1984, exactly as Moore's first *Swamp Thing* issues were being published on the other side of the Atlantic. It's tempting to think that they provided Moore with a safety valve – whereas *Swamp Thing* was slow, dark and intense, D.R. & Quinch's adventures were frenetic and hilarious. The strip charted the adventures of D.R. ("Diminished Responsibilities") and his large cohort, EE Quinch, a pair of juvenile delinquents who created mayhem and devastation wherever they went, and weren't above using nuclear weapons to liven things up. It drew comparisons with *The Young Ones* at the time, and nowadays looks like a precursor to the *Bill And Ted* movies. Often laugh-out-loud funny, it's a good demonstration of Moore's versatility, especially if read alongside the later instalments of *V for Vendetta* and early *Swamp Thing* stories he must have been working on at the same time. That said, it's possibly Moore's best-constructed series to that point – there are some elaborate set-ups and pay-offs, foreshadowing, parallel narratives, along with a number of other sly storytelling tricks. Both D.R. and Quinch take turns to narrate chapters of the story, and it's here Moore hones his skill of telling us one thing, while the picture tells quite another story. The captions assure us everything is fine, while the pictures usually depict a scene of absolute chaos.

The other series is considered by many to be among the best to appear in *2000AD*'s history, no mean feat when the comic has been a home for some of the great characters of British comics and launched many a star-studded career. Most *2000AD* characters – Judge Dredd, Strontium Dog, Rogue Trooper, Robohunter – have been cauldrons of testosterone, ones with jobs that involved not just carrying large guns, but using them at least twice on every page. The key to these characters' success was action: faces got kicked, buildings blew up and rampaging robots, vicious mutants and ugly aliens had their head blown off in every episode. It's a simple, effective formula, and many of *2000AD*'s current problems stem from forgetting the appeal of it, at a point when virtually every action film in the world has discovered the joys of combining colourful science fiction with gratuitous violence.

The Ballad Of Halo Jones was conceived by Moore as the complete opposite of the typical *2000AD* series, although Moore was not abandoning the *2000AD* formula, simply subverting it. The choice of artist was Ian Gibson, a stalwart of the magazine, who'd drawn Judge Dredd, Robohunter and a number of other regular and one-off strips. So *Halo Jones* looked like *2000AD*. It sounded like it too. One of the distinctive traits of *2000AD* is its futuristic slang – in a comic at least nominally aimed at children, there is an obvious practical reason why Judge Dredd exclaims "Drokk!" or "Grud!" at moments of stress; each weekly issue began with "Borag Thungg!," the traditional Betelgeusian greeting from the traditional Betelgeusian editor, Tharg. This unique vocabulary had, over the years, steadily grown to the point that it became a tradition, every six months or so, to publish a half-page glossary of Betelgeusian terms. Moore took this eccentricity to a new height, making the first six-page instalment of Halo Jones almost incomprehensible. The first line sets the tone: "dataday, day-to-day, making a pact with the facts … I'm swifty frisko, hi! algae baron lux roth chop: will he or won't he? is intervention his intention? over to jazz firpo at chop towers in pseudoportugal." And there are no concessions to the audience, no handy captions or notes from the editor – as there would normally be in the magazine – explaining what is going on. Indeed, many of the people reading the recap at the start of Book Two must have been grateful to have a few things set straight.

In a break with tradition, the protagonist was a woman; until Halo, the only major female character in *2000AD* was Judge Dredd supporting character Psi-Judge Anderson, who was not to get her own series until 1985. Not only that, but Halo was no super-competent amazon or a leather-clad cop with psi-powers, just an ordinary girl. As for her job … she didn't have one. She was an Increased Leisure Citizen, one of the long-term unemployed written off by the government and living, along with millions of other ILCs, on the Hoop, a vast complex floating in the Atlantic, out of sight and out of mind. The ten-year-olds who had bought the first issue of *2000AD* were schoolleavers now, and they were entering a Britain where factories were closing and two or three million were already unemployed. Judge Dredd had always been underpinned with dark satire: Mega-City One's pandemic crime and the near-total unemployment of its human population had always been implicitly linked. But in *Halo Jones*, the readers were identifying with the unemployed characters, not the lawmen keeping them in line.

The result is a piece of science fiction world building which mixes the surreal with the mundane, the casual mention that dolphins now rule the Earth with a shopping trip. There's an attention to detail in the strip, a consistency that rewards close attention on the readers' part (for example, although it's never explicitly stated, the people of this future seem to have adopted a Vegan diet). But the secret of the strip's success is Halo Jones herself, an everyman character with the simplest of goals – just to get away from her mundane existence. The first book sees her in awe of a beautiful spaceliner, Clara Pandy, which has been brought to the Hoop to be broken up for scrap. Inspired by the sight of the liner, and the brutal murder of a flatmate, Halo decides to leave, and when the Clara Pandy is saved and relaunched, she is on board, as a waitress, with her robot dog Toby. The second book is an almost traditional space adventure, with a murder mystery and an enigmatic passenger behind a locked door. Outside the confines of the ship, war is brewing, and Halo finds herself drawn into interstellar politics, and for Book Three, Moore brings the strip back to the heartland of *2000AD*, with a Future War story that takes the certainties of *Rogue Trooper* or *Judge Dredd* and deconstructs them for the Falklands generation.

Halo Jones became a minor cultural icon, inspiring the Transvision Vamp song *Hanging Out With Halo Jones*, the name of the band Halo James, and earning a name-check on 'Malaria,' the opening track on Shriekback's *Oil and Gold* album.

Book Four was promised (with suggestions at the time that there would be ten Books in total), and the prologue to Book Two set out what the future had in store for Halo Jones: a meeting with someone called Sally Quasa, and Halo Jones heading out "past Vega, past Moulquet and Lambard. She saw places that aren't even there any more" until she became a legend. But further books weren't forthcoming. Although Moore drew up plans for a Judge Dredd-related strip 'Badlander' (about a Judge's active retirement in the mutant infested Cursed Earth outside the city walls of Mega City One), for a potential Judge Dredd spin-off title it was clear he'd outgrown *2000AD*. 1985 was Moore's breakthrough year in the States, the year when his work on *Swamp Thing* was coming to public attention and he was starting to get regular work on other titles, while talking to DC management about some grand future projects. British comics publishers at the time offered nothing in the way of creators' rights or royalties. The industry was forced to change – in no small part due to the emergence of a generation of creators like Moore with the ability to sell comics on the strength of their name and who promptly accepted work in America where the conditions were better, although still far from perfect. With *2000AD*, Moore did not own the characters he'd created, nor could he prevent his material from being reprinted elsewhere, or otherwise exploited.

In issue 500 a number of prominent *2000AD* creators contribute to the story 'Tharg's Head Revisited.' On Moore and Gibson's page, the editor of *2000AD* comes looking for news of Book Four. Halo Jones grabs him – "Book Four? You're jestering! Not till you learn the right way to treat a lady! I mean you're not concerned who takes us out ... we could end up being sold to white slavers or dirty book dealers for all you care! We do all the work, but who is it who ends up with all the loot? Honestly! Living off the earnings of women! There's a name for people like you!" And that isn't even the most vitriolic attack in a quite extraordinary 'celebration.' *2000AD* had featured early work, and some of the best work, from a generation of British writers and artists, but with the terms the magazine offered, they just couldn't keep hold of their talent. Although the situation has changed and the magazine still appears every week, it has never quite recovered either artistically or in terms of sales from the departure of its best creators.

In the special *2000AD* issue 2001 (December 2000), *Halo Jones* is honoured with a two-page feature, extraordinary for a character who only appeared in 37 (of over 1,250) issues. The article ends by saying "Unfortunately, there are currently no plans for Halo's return – but never say never." The anonymous writer knows that, even over fifteen years late, *Halo Jones* Book Four and the return of her creator would bring more readers back to the fold than just about anything else *2000AD* could offer. Stranger things have happened, but if Book Four is going to appear, it will do so very much on Moore's terms – *2000AD* need him far more than he needs them.

3. America

Working for American comics publishers offered a number of attractions for Alan Moore. First of all, the market was bigger and supported more titles (the alternative at IPC was to write football strips for *Roy of the Rovers* or humour for *Buster* or *Whizzer & Chips*); secondly the pay was better and a royalty system existed so if sales improved the creators were rewarded; and thirdly, he was going to be in with a chance to play with the big, iconic characters like Superman and Batman. Finally and, as it turned out, most importantly, he would be allowed more creative freedom and his editors would allow him more room to experiment. Comics in Britain had traditionally been seen purely as a medium for the entertainment of children, an attitude only just changing as Moore left *2000AD*. In America, the big companies, particularly DC where Moore started out, knew there was a solid university and young adult audience still buying comics and were willing to stretch the boundaries a little more to cater for them.

Swamp Thing

Swamp Thing was not one of DC's prestigious titles. The character was fairly well established, having first appeared in the horror anthology title *House Of Secrets* (Issue 92, June 1971), and in his own title a year later, which ran for four years. He had been revived in 1982 to capitalise on the release of the Wes Craven-directed movie (which subsequently spawned a sequel and a TV series). Despite this, *Swamp Thing* had never been a high-profile or high-sales title. Moore took it over with Issue 20 (January 1984) without any fuss or promotion. Even regular readers would not have found anything particular to get excited about in the story. As the title suggests, 'Loose Ends' is a deft clearing of the decks, Moore shutting down a few sub-plots from previous issues. It has never been reprinted.

Issue 21's story 'The Anatomy Lesson' is where Moore really sets to work, and the first thing he does changes and expands the potential of his lead character no end. It had previously been established that the Swamp Thing was created when scientist Alec Holland, working on a 'bio-restorative formula,' had been caught in an explosion and fallen into a swamp, somehow merging with the plant life there. For the previous ten or so years, most *Swamp Thing* stories had revolved around Alec's attempts to regain his humanity – a fairly limited ploy, if for no other reason that the series would come to an end if he succeeded. Moore moved the goalposts

– Swamp Thing, it was discovered, wasn't a half-man, half-plant creature, he was a plant that had somehow absorbed Holland's memories. He couldn't regain his human body … it wasn't ever part of the mix. Swamp Thing was a "ghost dressed in weeds." It seemed like a minor tweak of a secret origin, but it shifted the emphasis away from a simple desire to turn back the clock and towards a broader exploration of what it meant to be human. Swamp Thing could never go back; from now on he would be set apart from the human world, and would have to discover how he fitted into the grand scheme of things.

Moore's run on the series lasted roughly three years, and can be broken down into roughly three phases. From issue 21 to issue 36, Moore runs simple but effective self-contained horror stories, rarely more than a couple of issues long, while establishing a growing love between Abby Cable (an existing character who soon became a Moore everywoman like Liz Moran) and Swamp Thing. They consummate their relationship in the extraordinary 'Rites Of Spring' in issue 34, surely the first comic to exclusively focus on a sex act between members of different natural kingdoms. It was an indication just how far Moore had brought the title in his first year: it had a gorgeous painted cover at a time when that was extremely rare, it won Eagle Awards and it earned a lot of attention for the series. All just in time for the second phase: issue 37 saw the beginning of the ambitious *American Gothic* storyline as Swamp Thing explored the underside of American life in the company of the enigmatic John Constantine (while issue 37 is Constantine's official first appearance, he had appeared in a crowd scene in issue 25 – an indication that Moore had clear plans for the direction of the series almost from day one). Constantine was created by Moore as a "blue collar" magician, one who looks a lot like the singer Sting, or at least he did until the DC legal people got nervous. Constantine was an English working-class lad, and proved very popular, graduating to his own title, *Hellblazer*, in 1987 which is still going strong. In *American Gothic*, Constantine is preparing Swamp Thing for a confrontation with ultimate darkness, culminating, in issue 50, with an epic battle between the forces of Heaven and Hell.

This was followed by a powerful epilogue as Swamp Thing returned to the material world to discover Abby had been charged with "crimes against nature" for her relationship with him; skipping bail, she was rearrested in Gotham City. At the end of the double-length issue 53, Swamp Thing is destroyed … and the third phase begins, as Abby tries to rebuild her life. A couple of months passed before Swamp Thing reappeared, on a distant planet. He then spent almost a year heading home, via a number of exotic worlds.

By accident or fate's design, *Swamp Thing* was the perfect vehicle for Moore. The series had always been set on the fringes of the regular DC Universe, the same place that Superman, Batman and Wonder Woman lived. This allowed Moore to pull in guest stars (and with them, casual readers who might follow those characters, but not normally Swamp Thing) from time to time, but gave him a good excuse not to have a constant superhero presence, as happened in many other DC titles. It was a superhero title only when it wanted to be. As a horror comic, it gave Moore access to a menagerie of occult characters – magicians, demons and ghosts – from more mainstream comics, giving a sense of a wider world. While exploring alien worlds, Moore gets a chance to revisit and revamp a number of DC characters with a science fiction background, like Adam Strange.

Swamp Thing had a number of artists during Moore's run. That can often be a problem for a running title – it's a collaborative medium, after all. Different artists can be confusing and lead to inconsistencies. It makes it very difficult to build momentum – and the "look" of a comic is very important in attracting new readers. But *Swamp Thing* had a definite house style, following Stephen Bissette and John Totlenben's lead. The unsung star of the series was colourist Tatjana Wood. Her work is one good reason to track down the original comics, not the reprints – she creates a murky world, where colours merge and bleed together into the newsprint pages. Current comics and trade paperbacks are printed on better paper – and as the inks don't soak into the pages, Wood's colours appear too bright and too well-defined.

Nowadays, a lot of comics look like *Swamp Thing*. There's a whole range of DC comics, the Vertigo imprint, telling horror stories set in the seamier parts of the contemporary world, using characters and themes from legends and religion. They use, indeed often rely on, "adult themes" – gore and mild nudity. But when it first came out, there was nothing on the newsstands quite like it, and Vertigo became a focus for fans looking for more grown-up comics.

The Vertigo imprint offered others the chance to do what Moore had already bought to his particular tributary off the mainstream DC Universe and tell some offbeat superhero stories. In an early issue (24), the Justice League of America, a team of all the top DC heroes, watches from the sidelines as Swamp Thing fights (old Atom and Green Lantern minor villain) the Floronic Man. We never hear Superman's name, his face is kept in shadows, we just hear him described as "a man who can see across the planet and wring diamonds from its anthracite" (that last talent was rarely seen in the comics, but made for a memorable scene in the movie *Superman III* – Moore's referring to what the mass audience would know, even if they'd never read a Superman comic). It was a new take on familiar, perhaps over-familiar, material. Moore was restoring some of the sense of wonder to old characters, without getting bogged down in the minutiae. While superheroes might seem incongruous, these are characters who are well known to the general public. Issue 53 sees Swamp Thing facing off against Batman (the issue appeared as *Dark Knight Returns* was first being published), and while a general audience might recognise the name, and the costume, this wasn't the Adam West version of the character, but a complex man, a compassionate hero, but one who won't for any reason permit his city to be destroyed.

Moore did guest spots for other comics during this time – often fill-in stories with a simple twist, work akin to his *2000AD* Future Shocks. But there were more substantial pieces, like a *Vigilante* two-parter dealing with domestic violence. In 1985 he collaborated with Dave Gibbons on 'For The Man Who Has Everything,' one of the greatest Superman stories ever told – and reprinted as such with the other contenders for the title in a DC trade paperback of that name. Wonder Woman, Batman and Robin visit Superman at his home, the Fortress of Solitude, to give him birthday presents only to find that the alien warlord Mongul has got there first and incapacitated Superman with an alien fungus that has put Superman into a dream state, where he gets his heart's desire ... an ordinary life on a Krypton that was never destroyed. The story intercuts between that dream, where Superman has a wife and children, and the reality, with a slam-bang fight that also acts as a tour of the Fortress. From his *Swamp Thing* work, you'd perhaps expect a more down-to-Earth story from Moore, one dealing with a "real life" issue. And that, when it comes down to it, is what you get: the story contains a rare insight into Superman's psyche, we get to see him celebrate his birthday with his best friends. But Moore isn't scared of dealing with traditional superheroics – the fight scenes in the story are as good as they get, the fantasy and science fiction elements are brought into the foreground.

By the time Moore's run on *Swamp Thing* ended, the series had won most of comics' top awards, and had gone from being a struggling second-string character to one of DC's top-selling titles – monthly sales rose from about 17,000 to over 100,000. If Moore could do that to *Swamp Thing*, DC realised, then the sky would be the limit if he was given more popular characters to work on, or was able to create characters of his own. As in Britain, the comics audience in America was getting older, more sophisticated and had a higher disposable income than had once been the case. Unlike the British companies, the American publishers had the money to capitalise on this (DC was then a division of Warners, now the multi-tentacled AOL Time Warner). Comics started to appear on better paper, the fan favourites were collected in trade paperback editions. DC, in particular, began a comprehensive overhaul of their ranges, a "back to basics" approach, one identical to that done by Moore on *Marvelman* and *Swamp Thing*. Moore was hardly the only figure involved in this process, but would remain a key player.

Moore discussed a lot of other projects with DC. Early on, he expressed an interest in writing the *Justice League Of America* or *The Metal Men*. There was talk of a *Martian Manhunter* series, taking the character back to its roots of McCarthyite fifties America. On various occasions, Moore mentioned that he wanted to write a *Challengers Of The Unknown* series and was planning a three-part *Lois Lane* mini-series, as well as a *Tommy Tomorrow* series with Dave Gibbons. He and Kevin O'Neill worked on a four-part *Bizarro World* series, which was apparently spiked after *Superman* was revamped and his old villain Bizarro was written out of official DC continuity. Moore also discussed a *Mr Monster/Swamp Thing* crossover.

The Killing Joke

Even before *Swamp Thing* hit its stride, Moore had been signed up to write a Batman story, a prestige project that would be printed in a format that did justice to the work. It was a collaboration with the artist Brian Bolland, who'd actually made the move from the UK to America before Moore and had scored a big hit drawing the series *Camelot 3000*, which saw the Arthurian myths retold in a futuristic setting, and which had been aimed squarely at the direct market – specialised comics shops rather than the traditional news-stand distributors. Originally, Bolland had wanted to do a story where Batman met Judge Dredd (a character Bolland had made his own in *2000AD*), but that fell through. Instead, a new story was conceived, a battle between Batman and his arch-enemy the Joker, *The Killing Joke*. The story had a long production history, and the comic eventually appeared in 1988, after *Watchmen*, around the time Moore was finishing off *V For Vendetta*. At the height of his fame, in fact.

The Killing Joke was hugely successful, and it was a big influence on the Tim Burton *Batman* films, but truth to tell, it's not actually a very good example of Moore's work. The Brian Bolland artwork is lovely. The story does some important things to Batman – establishing an origin for the Joker; setting out that the Joker and Batman are both insane in their way ("two sides of the same coin," a phrase that quickly passed from great insight to cliché); and it sees the end of Batgirl, as her alter ego Barbara Gordon is shot and paralysed by the Joker (he also sexually assaults her, although later Batman comics have steered clear of reminding their readers of that). Like Frank Miller's *Dark Knight Returns* and *Batman: Year One, Killing Joke* became a cornerstone of the Batman myth. While he's doing big things with Batman continuity in particular, Moore knows he's playing with the core concepts of all superhero/supervillain battles – good versus evil, law versus crime, control versus chaos. Moore doesn't even name his hero or villain in the story – everyone reading it knows who they are. But at heart, as Moore himself has pointed out, *The Killing Joke* isn't saying anything interesting about the human condition. The central premise, that one bad day is enough to turn a normal man into a psychotic like the Joker (or the Batman), just doesn't apply to the real world, where people don't become clown-themed criminals if they fall into a vat of chemicals (or decide to fight crime dressed as a bat because one flies in through the window). Moore's portrayal of the Batman as someone intent on rehabilitating the Joker, convinced he can be redeemed, is much more interesting, and there are hints that the Joker retains just enough sanity to realise Batman's wrong, and there isn't any hope for him. But the theme isn't developed enough. In the end it looks lovely, but it's a rare example of a Moore story where the art is better than the writing.

Watchmen

Chances are, if you're reading this book, you've read *Watchmen*. If not, then put this book down and go and find a copy, read it, then come back.

Watchmen is the *Citizen Kane* of comics, a vast, innovative work that regularly tops 'best of' lists. Like *Citizen Kane*, some of the innovations have become familiar, even cliché, after many years of imitation. Like *Citizen Kane*, if there is a complaint it's that the technique is more sophisticated and compelling than the story. Technically, *Watchmen* is perfect. A story about a chain of cause and effect, the plans and mechanisms that control the world, the structure of the story runs like clockwork. Tiny details build up to make a bigger picture, patterns and images recur; the

39

essence of the story can, in retrospect, be extrapolated from the central panel on the first page of the first issue: the sentiments expressed by the narrator unite Rorschach and Ozymandias – they both see the end of the world as imminent – it's just an issue of choice. The street in New York is awash with blood; the character who turns out to be Rorschach leaves his own bloody trail; his direction is opposite to that of the truck belonging to Adrian Veidt …

It's a method of storytelling all but impossible in any other medium. The series represents a fusion of all the techniques Moore had been using in his various strips to date. Like *V For Vendetta*, each page is laid out with grids of regular panels (unlike *V*, these widen out when the story demands it); like *Swamp Thing*, scenes are often linked with a telling phrase or image; like D.R. & Quinch, the words often jar with the pictures – what we're being told is going on is not what we see; like *Halo Jones* a whole world is built up from incidental details – what people eat and wear, what they watch on TV; like *Marvelman*, the presence of superheroes has a profound effect on the world.

It's 1985. Since the fifties, the world has been changed by the presence of Dr Manhattan, an American scientist who fell into a particle accelerator and re-emerged capable of transmuting matter into any form, and with a memory that allows him to see the future as easily as the past. At first, Manhattan was co-opted into a rather sad band of "costumed heroes" who thought they could solve crime. None of these had superpowers as such, although Ozymandias is exceptionally intelligent, and the Comedian is exceptionally skilled in the use of weapons. Gradually, though, Manhattan changes the world – his powers have allowed airships and electric cars to become a reality. He also proved decisive in Vietnam, winning the war for America, allowing Nixon to be re-elected. The Comedian, working for the CIA, has also helped US domestic and foreign politics along via a string of assassinations and covert ops. The result is that the cold war has deepened, Nixon is still president and the world is perpetually on the brink of nuclear war. The story starts with the Comedian's murder – someone is killing masked heroes, and setting in motion a series of events that could mean the end of the world.

The story, ultimately, is so straightforward it is almost banal. The identity of the Comedian's murderer is, within a few issues, so obvious that you wonder if the twist is going to be that it isn't him. The resolution of the story seems a little too neat – the American and Russian governments react just as the "villain" wants them to, by ending the Cold War, but that's by no means the only thing they could have done in the circumstances. But any complaints are nit-picking. Nothing is perfect, *Watchmen* comes a lot closer to it than just about anything else. Moore is clearly in complete command of the medium – while his early *Marvelman* and *Swamp Thing* scripts were text-heavy, often using rather purple prose, by now he's learnt when not to say anything, and there are whole sequences without dialogue. There are plenty of comic book conventions that aren't there, too – sound effect captions, thought balloons, captions from an omniscient narrator. Gibbons' art is intricate, deceptively simple. The devil is in the detail, and just about every panel of *Watchmen* is packed with it, from visual motifs, clues to the mystery, to some beautifully thought-through set dressing. In this world Heinz has 58 varieties. The phrase 'Who Watches the Watchmen?' appears scrawled on walls throughout the city – but we never see the whole phrase in one panel. The panels are almost fractal – every time you look at them, there's a detail you didn't spot the first time, there are hints at new patterns.

Watchmen was quickly optioned for a film and a script was written by Sam Hamm, who wrote the first *Batman* movie. Terry Gilliam was to direct. In the end, it's probably just as well it didn't appear – while Gilliam seemed the perfect candidate to bring such a detailed alternate Earth to the big screen, he worried that a four hundred-page labyrinthine story just couldn't be condensed into a two-hour film. While Moore himself didn't seem unduly concerned, rumours that Arnold Schwarzenegger had been approached to play quantum physicist Dr Manhattan had fanboy alarm bells ringing. Bootlegs of Hamm's script have long been available to collectors, and make for pretty grim reading. A new action sequence has been bolted onto the beginning, presumably to start the movie with a bang … but it strikes a crass note from the first page (one of the first lines is a SWAT captain declaring "Christ almighty, it's the goddamned Watchmen!"). A lot of the subtlety has been lost, and in some cases with it has gone the whole point of scenes. Hamm changes Moore's dialogue, not always to its benefit. At the end of Chapter Seven of the comic, for example, there's the following exchange:

LAURIE: Dan, was tonight good? Did you like it?
DREIBERG: Uh-huh.
LAURIE: Did the costumes make it good? Dan?
DREIBERG: Yeah. Yeah, I guess the costumes had something to do with it. It just feels strange, you know? To come out and admit that to somebody. To come out of the closet.

While this is a post-coital scene, it's ambiguous what the 'it' refers to – Laurie and Dreiberg have just made love (for the first time, Dreiberg has previously proved unable to rise to the occasion). But before that, Laurie and Dreiberg have spent the night being superheroes, rescuing people from a fire. Dreiberg has conquered more than one form of impotence this evening by donning his old superhero costume. The same scene in the movie script runs:

LAURIE: I bet I know what made the difference this time.

DREIBERG: What?

LAURIE: *(smirking)* The costumes. Am I right?

[DREIBERG seems mildly shocked by the proposition. Then, despite himself, he starts to chortle. She pokes him playfully on the arm.]

LAURIE (cont.): Come on. Admit it!

DREIBERG: No way. I'm not *that* much of a pervert.

It's the opposite message, a far more conventional, unproblematic one. He might need to dress as an owl to get it up, but heaven forfend he might be a *pervert*. The playfulness, gentleness, double meaning, eroticism and even the economy of Moore's dialogue are altered into something that seems to exactly miss the point of the original.

In the end, *Watchmen*'s narrative tricks are novel for comics, but nothing special in cinema – *Watchmen*'s method of going into flashbacks, of staying on one character and cutting to him in the past in the same pose would be cinematic cliché, not an innovation. So much of *Watchmen* depends on the detail, the subtlety, the wordplay, the juxtaposition of images. On the big screen all of that would be stripped away, leaving just a rather straightforward story.

Watchmen was a phenomenal success, and received the unprecedented honour of a trade paperback collection within a month of the last issue appearing. Along with *Dark Knight Returns*, it became the focus of media coverage of what was happening in comics. It was the first comic book to win a Hugo Award. There was talk of a one-shot *Minutemen* prequel, and maybe even a genuine *Tales Of The Black Freighter* one-shot, but these don't seem to have been developed very far.

Twilight Of The Superheroes

Moore was approached to write for films and television. In 1988, he wrote a script for Malcolm McLaren, *Fashion Beast*, an updating of *Beauty And The Beast* set in the fashion world. McLaren liked the script, but finance fell through. The same year, he was offered the chance to write the twenty-fifth anniversary *Doctor Who* story, but declined. The producers of *Robocop 2* wanted Moore to write the script (when he turned it down, the honour went to Frank Miller).

Moore was, for the moment at least, still interested in superhero comics. In fact, he proposed an epic superhero crossover tale to DC in 1987. Crossovers between different comic titles had been popular for years – if Batman appeared in a Superman comic, then some of Batman's fans would buy it that month. It was the logic that had led to Moore writing a fair few crossovers as part of his *Swamp Thing* range. In the eighties, one series would take this idea to an extreme. The twelve-part *Crisis On Infinite Earths* by Marv Wolfman and artist George Perez celebrated DC's fiftieth anniversary in 1985 by involving every single DC character, past, present and future in one universe-threatening story. It went further – every comics title was to have at least one issue that was a '*Crisis* crossover' (*Swamp Thing*'s was in issue 46). It encouraged people to give different titles a try (although, paradoxically, *Crisis* crossovers weren't typical examples of any book). *Crisis* was a huge success, and was a useful mechanism to hurry the revamping of the whole of DC's output. Marvel had already had the similar *Secret Wars*, and since then, every summer both companies have tended to have vast 'crossover events' that involve most of their superhero titles for a month or two. At their best, they can be exciting and epic ... more typically, they seem to be an imposed interruption on the runs of otherwise perfectly good comics.

Moore pitched *Twilight Of The Superheroes* with these problems in mind. It would be set twenty or thirty years in the future, and would set up the 'rules' for time travel in the DC universe – incidentally allowing a few continuity glitches to be smoothed over. The story was wide-ranging ... starting in 1987, where John Constantine is warned of a nightmare future, where the superheroes are fighting a brutal civil war having come to rule the world almost as feudal lords. The superheroes have grouped into clans, or Houses, such as the House of Steel (Superman and his allies, including his wife Wonder Woman) and the House of Thunder (Captain Marvel and the Marvel Family). A marriage between the two houses threatens to create a new super-elite, and the other superheroes (and the surviving villains) team up to bring both Houses down. This leads to a bloody battle, in which many superheroes are killed … and leaves Earth open to attack from aliens. The future Constantine has to use all his guile to repel the alien invasion and (shades of *V For Vendetta*) leaves the world without a government, but with vigilantes like Batman and the Shadow to ensure order. The final scene, back in the present, sees Constantine shocked by the actions of his future self.

Moore's proposal document sprawls almost as much as the final story would have. It's quite a radical idea (albeit one that's clearly been influenced by *Dark Knight Returns*). Unfortunately, Moore left DC over the ratings dispute and the series was never written, although over the years, apparently quite independently of Moore, various DC creators have come to the same conclusions he did. "Hypertime" has been invented to explain that all the Batman stories you read "happen" somewhere. Most significantly, the series *Kingdom Come* (1997, Mark Waid, art: Alex Ross) was set twenty or thirty years in a dystopian future and saw the last days of the superheroes, not to mention the ultimate battle between Superman and Captain Marvel, a romantic relationship between Superman and Wonder Woman and a crucial role for a shadowy, hidden Batman.

Boom!

Alan Moore tired of the comics revolution before most. By the time his *Swamp Thing* run was drawing to an end, he was increasingly disenchanted with the way things were going. *Watchmen* had sold in huge numbers and had made him a rich man for the first time in his life – but his royalty rate meant, according to some reports, that he and Gibbons ended up with only something like 2% between them of the amount DC made as publishers, and they got little or nothing from merchandising, like the portfolios, badges or even the movie options. There was little doubt by now that Moore had a following, but others were benefiting more than he was from his work and name.

At least as importantly, he felt his creativity was being restricted at DC. Early on, he'd been pleased that Karen Berger, his editor on *Swamp Thing*, had allowed more controversial or adult material through, even fought his corner on occasion. The last straw came when DC announced (without, it seems, consulting their creative staff) that from now on the more adult books would carry a "For Mature Readers" warning. It was perhaps a sensible move – *Swamp Thing* shared shelves with *Care Bears* and *ALF* comics, the Christian right were a political force, and the growing publicity given to comics for adults meant a moral backlash was likely (in the event, it never came, at least not in the organised, sustained way it had in the fifties). In an environment where comics are commonly seen as purely for children, it was always going to be easier to change the labels on comics than public perception of the whole genre. Perhaps, although he never said this, Moore relished the thought of a run-in with the 'moral majority' – it rarely does any harm to sales or critical reception if there are people burning your books or boycotting your films in the Bible Belt. Moore's given argument was that he was writing books, and books didn't have such a rating system. He also thought that a rating system would encourage writers to play up to the rating, as perhaps happens in cinema – running scared of even the most innocuous 'problematic' material in the lower ratings, including gratuitous sex and violence in the higher ones (he suggested that instead of "For Mature Readers," DC might like to use the label "Full of Tits and Innards"). In many ways he was prophetic – DC and Marvel both have ranges, Vertigo and Marvel Max, that are for mature readers and have often fallen into the trap of a rather self-conscious drugs 'n' sex 'n' swearing approach.

For a long time, Moore had been suggesting that it would be better for editors not to publish material they couldn't justify artistically, rather than come up with an excuse to do so. Now, as Moore saw it, DC's plans would mean he was being shunted away into a ghetto. Moore objected, both publicly and privately, but as he refused to work with Marvel, and the British comics and independent sector in America couldn't afford him, DC executives must have assumed he would settle down. After all, where else could he go?

The answer, as anyone who'd read *Halo Jones* could have told them, was simple. He went out.

4. The Wilderness Years

Anyone could be forgiven for thinking that Alan Moore had vanished off the face of the earth.

Moore had always been prolific and a highly visible figure in the world of comics. But there was surprisingly little new from him after he left *Swamp Thing* in September 1987 and the last issue of *Watchmen* a month later. For a while, this lack of new material was masked by the appearance of some long-term projects: *The Killing Joke*, the reprinting and completion of *Miracleman* and *V For Vendetta*, not to mention a frenzied reprinting and repackaging of almost all his earlier work in one form or another, from cheap American fix-ups of his *2000AD* work, to the more lavish appearance of some unpublished *Warrior* work in *A1*. Moore helped out a fair few worthy projects by writing introductions or the odd short strip, but seemed to be doing little in the way of new work.

Having severed his ties with DC, Moore announced that, along with his wife Phyllis and their mutual lover Deborah Delano, he was setting up Mad Love, an imprint that would publish his own work. Moore also signed up to write two ambitious running strips for *Taboo*, an anthology comic which, as the name suggested, was a conscious attempt to stretch the boundaries of the medium. He was also the first person publishers turned to when they were looking to start publishing graphic novels.

If all had gone to plan, Moore might have been able to change the face of comics and shift them into the mainstream market – none of the work he was planning involved superheroes, or even science fiction. Had this new wave of his work appeared reliably and regularly in the first couple of years of the nineties, as originally intended, it is possible that the readers brought to comics by *Watchmen* and *Dark Knight* would have stayed, and that Moore would have inspired a few more creators to follow his lead. Unfortunately, all the big projects he embarked on as he left were destined to be subject to delays and cancellation. The graphic novel revolution also proved to be a false start: slow to commit, by the time major publishers had their books in the shops, the moment had passed; the bookstores were already swamped with superhero and science fiction reprints so the new better quality lines made little impact. They were expensive at a time when speculators wanted to buy cheap, sell dear.

But, at the height of his fame and commercial and critical success in late 1987, early 1988, Moore couldn't possibly have foreseen that. And it's here that some of Moore's most interesting, sophisticated and truly innovative work was done.

Politics

Moore realised that people would listen to what he had to say, and his work became more overtly political, focussing on specific governments and policies, rather than the bigger pictures encompassed by *V For Vendetta* or *Watchmen*, or the rather generalised anti-pollution, anti-weapons manufacturers' greed stance that informs much of *Swamp Thing*. This new focus is reflected in his mainstream work. The prospect of nuclear war – particularly the philosophy behind Mutually Assured Destruction – plays a crucial part of the world-view of *Watchmen*. In the last issue of *Miracleman*, our hero and his allies dismantle the apparatus of the nation states … in a single page. Nuclear weapons go in one panel, Thatcher in another. In the next panel, Miracleman abolishes money.

But Moore also started to write in support of specific causes. The first book published by Mad Love, *AARGH!*, was an anthology book in which the top names from the comics field got together to protest (with wildly varying degrees of artistic success, it has to be said) against the government's then-new Clause 28, which promised to ban local councils from "promoting homosexuality." Moore's own contribution, 'The Mirror Of Love,' is a typical Moore 'long view' story, like V's lecture to mankind or Gull's tour of London in *From Hell*, in which contemporary prejudices and attitudes are seen as recent developments in the grand scheme of things. Homosexuality has always been with us, history has benefited immensely from the contribution of homosexuals.

Around the same time, Moore wrote 'Shadowplay: The Secret Team,' one half of *Brought To Light*, "a graphic docudrama" exposing covert CIA drug smuggling and arms dealing, based on a lawsuit brought by the Christic Institute. In these post-Irangate, post-*X-Files*, post-Clinton times *Brought To Light*'s assertion that the American intelligence services have been running secret operations for decades and have operated above the law, effectively serving as a shadow government, is almost commonplace. Reading 'Shadowplay' now, it's hard to believe that the audience at the time could be surprised by any of the revelations, however horrific. It's our loss – Moore brings home the horror of seeing literally millions of people murdered as a result of American foreign activity. It's a clever piece of writing – polemic, but never as over the top or absurd as the events being depicted. That said, 'Shadowplay' doesn't quite work as a comic strip – the idea of having the narrator as an American eagle works, and Sienkiewicz's art is murky and evocative, but the strip is essentially an illustrated monologue. Moore has performed the piece (to music by

Gary Lloyd), and it's got far more momentum that way – as originally presented, the pictures almost get in the way of the story.

Big Numbers

The early nineties saw Moore take the playful, postmodern approach he'd brought to superheroes, along with this more explicit political agenda out into the wider world of society and urban myth.

The first Mad Love series to be announced was *The Mandlebrot Set*. It was going to be an ambitious twelve-part series, set in contemporary Britain, and it was to be painted by fan-favourite artist Bill Sienkiewicz, veteran of *X-Men* spin-off *The New Mutants* and the artist of Frank Miller's *Elektra* series (and Moore's collaborator on 'Shadowplay'). The title changed to *Big Numbers*, and the first issue appeared in April 1990.

Set in Hampton, a hardly-disguised version of Moore's native Northampton, the first two issues introduce us to the cast. The lead character is Christine Gathercole, a poet and novelist, who's returning to her home-town to write a new novel. We meet her family, her friends and a few local characters, including a number of the mentally ill who are part of the 'care in the community' project. Meanwhile, in Los Angeles, a group of American businessmen plan a vast shopping and office complex for Hampton. From the scale model, it's clear it will represent as great an imposition on the people of the city as Miracleman's palace did on London – and it looks just as alien. The series is, as its original title suggested, about life as chaos theory – how a small event can have large consequences, how it's impossible to plot out a life, because something will always turn up. How the big picture relates to the small.

And after that … we don't know. Moore had the whole story plotted out and had written five full scripts. We know that while the series started in black and white, it was to have ended in full colour – the second issue has the first splash of colour, in a single panel. Sienkiewicz quit the project, apparently completing at least some of Issue 3, after a number of delays. His assistant Al Columbia was brought in to take over, but didn't deliver his first issue, as planned, instead – comics legend has it – he did complete it, but chose either to destroy it or run off with it. It's unlikely to be completed in comics, but Moore has discussed developing it for television.

It's difficult to come to any judgement on *Big Numbers*. It's interesting that this is almost certainly the first Moore story that isn't melodrama. Christine is another in a long line of Moore's 'ordinary female' leads, but here she's a character in her own right, rather than a Lois Lane stuck in a story with the big boys. There are fantasy elements – dream sequences, hallucinations, even the SF trappings of the proposed shopping centre. But everything's small scale, it's about ordinary people, who do things for ordinary human reasons. The narrative shies away from the flashy jump cuts of *Watchmen* and *The Killing Joke*. Would *Big Numbers* have changed the face of comics? It might have done, it's impossible to say.

A Small Killing

A Small Killing was a full-length graphic novel published by Victor Gollancz, and now seems like a fragment from a parallel universe where comic books are published by mainstream publishers and are about real people. The irony being, of course, that because it's not science fiction or a superhero tale, it tends to be overlooked by Moore aficionados. It's the story of Timothy Hole, who (like Christine Gathercole in *Big Numbers* – and Moore at the time) returns from an acclaimed career to his roots. He's an advertising man, selling a diet drink to the Russians, agonising about the execution of the advertising campaign, but he's being followed by a sinister little boy.

A Small Killing might almost be considered a companion piece for its partial namesake *The Killing Joke*, or maybe some form of artistic response to it. They both deal with formative events of a man's life, viewing them in flashback and contrasting them with his current situation. Unlike *The Killing Joke*, here Moore's dealing with ordinary people in ordinary places, not the simplistic moral certainties of comics. It's quite possibly Moore's most underrated work, perhaps because on face value, it feels like a short film, or perhaps a television play. It's using the comics medium very cleverly, and Oscar Zarate's art is perfect for it – he creates a colourful London that's almost like a series of GLC-sponsored murals, allowing snarling caricatures and charming little details.

Lost Girls

One of two running series in the anthology series *Taboo*, *Lost Girls* again saw Moore taking comics, or at least mainstream comics, into new areas. As Moore had said in *Watchmen*, there was a long history of "Tijuana Bibles," crude comic strips that showed famous celebrities in lewd situations. *Lost Girls* was an attempt to widen the traditional scope of erotica, to create a literary version of the form. The comic strip is, when you think about it, the perfect medium to use. Moore's agenda was to create what might be called post-feminist pornography – one with strong female characters, one where the traditional confessional narrative of the Victorian erotic novel becomes linked to the feminist narrative of a young woman's growing self-awareness and empowerment, one where psychology and emotional involvement are as important as depiction of sex acts. The comic was so squarely aimed at female readers that it perhaps protests too much – Melinda Gebbie's flowing, pastel art is almost the definition of feminine.

It's 1913, and three women familiar from children's literature, Alice, Wendy and Dorothy, meet at a hotel by Lake Constance. They embark on a number of erotic encounters, with each other as well as other guests. Their childhood adventures are reimagined as formative sexual experiences – so, Dorothy's home is destroyed by a tornado as she experiences her first orgasm. Gebbie's art keeps everything sensual, however explicit things get. From the few chapters published so far *Lost Girls* is an experiment that seems to work. Moore and Gebbie are currently completing the series, to be published as a single, complete volume in 2002 – but by its very nature, it's never going to get the wide audience it deserves.

On the other hand, Moore's second series in *Taboo* could well become his most widely-known – it's the first that's made it to film.

From Hell

Moore started work on *From Hell* in 1988, exactly a century after the Jack the Ripper murders it portrays. Moore probably didn't imagine that it would be a decade before the last issue would appear. Jack the Ripper is not exactly virgin territory for writers, but Moore attempts perhaps the most ambitious tackling of the subject. *From Hell* uses fiction as a method of historical investigation. To understand the Jack the Ripper case, Moore contends, it's not enough to look at the dry facts. As the grandfather of modern conspiracy theories, a century's worth of contradictory and incomplete pieces of information has built up. Even at the time, though, the murder of five prostitutes was not unprecedented. We only remember it now because the Ripper's crimes caught the imagination of the contemporary press and the public. Right from the start, the crimes entered the realm of fiction, and the "reality" of the case has rarely been anything but a sideshow. *From Hell* is a postmodern detective story – reaching for a truth that can never be pinned down. It's Jack the Ripper for the *Twin Peaks* generation.

Moore takes one theory and develops it. It's not a whodunnit, we know who the Ripper is from the start. So: the prostitutes who were the Ripper's victims were aware of an illegitimate royal child. They were short of money, and jointly tried their hand at blackmail. On the explicit orders of Queen Victoria, the royal surgeon, Sir William Gull, is commissioned to eliminate the women. Gull, though, is insane – a high-ranking Mason, he has visions in which Jabulon, God, informs him of the patterns and greater purpose of his mission. Gull invests the murders with sacred significance and pursues the woman as a true zealot. Gull sees himself as protecting the whole of world civilisation. He becomes the first to understand that the symbolic importance of the murders is far more important than the mere events. Chapter Four is an early set piece – Gull takes his coachman and accomplice Netley on a tour of Victorian London. Certain churches and other places throughout London are invested with particular historical or symbolic meaning. Join the dots and it forms a pentagram, a magical sigil that has ensured the domination of patriarchy for centuries.

In the interests of research for this book, I followed the route set out in *From Hell* (accompanied by my friend, and sometime co-author, Mark Clapham). The churches designed by Nicholas Hawksmoor that mark points on the journey are, if anything, more incongruous and alien than Eddie Campbell's art suggests. Christchurch at Spitalfields, in particular, is a disturbing structure, not at all like a traditional church or the Victorian buildings around it (a contrast made all the more marked by being so close to Spitalfields market, which was built in 1887, the year before the murders). A couple of the points on the route, Battle Bridge Road and Hackney Fields, do seem arbitrary – including them seems to prove nothing except that if you mark a pentagram on a map, you'll end up with a pentagram. Except that's rather the point of *From Hell*. If you collect enough data, you can use it to discern all sorts of patterns, coincidences and historical echoes. In the epilogue to *From Hell*, 'Dance Of The Gull-Catchers,' Moore makes the message explicit – *From Hell* is a fiction, after several hundred pages assembling a compelling case that Gull was the Ripper, bringing to light a number of the anomalies and inconsistencies of the case, Moore tells us Gull almost certainly isn't the Ripper after all. Gull is a real person, a respected doctor (the first to identify the condition anorexia). Moore is fully aware that his examination of the Ripper murders, as with all the others, is a rather ignoble act – making money from the all too real murders of impoverished women, expressing prurient interest and encouraging the worst forms of voyeurism and exploitation. The women involved found it difficult to survive, but their murders have, over the years, made a lot of writers a lot of money.

Eddie Campbell's scratchy art brings contemporary newspaper engravings and scratched, faded Victorian photographs to life. At first, it seems inaccessible (most American comic books that can afford to be are in colour), but the effect becomes hypnotic, utterly absorbing. Anything more photorealistic would have made *From Hell* into just another horror comic.

Bust!

With a kinder publishing history, *From Hell* would have been instantly recognised as the important work it is. But Moore's output in the early nineties was characterised by abortive projects. Unfortunately, having cut himself off from the mainstream publishers, in a comics industry that was finding it difficult to sustain the growth of the late eighties, Moore's work became very vulnerable to the financial problems of his publishers. An early sign was the collapse of Eclipse. Moore's run on *Miracleman* was over by then, although it means that the collected editions have remained out of print.

Big Numbers only lasted two issues, *Taboo* managed seven, but folded with four-fifths of *From Hell* and *Lost Girls* untold. *From Hell* was picked up by Tundra, who reprinted the chapters from *Taboo*, as well as a handful more before hitting financial problems. The series then transferred to Kitchen Sink, but even then it was erratic – on average only two issues a year appeared from 1993. *Lost Girls* was also picked up by Kitchen Sink … but only reached two issues in 1995-96 before they too faltered.

The comics boom, and the resulting bursting of the bubble hit both independent and mainstream publishers hard. Even as the comics-as-accessories boom of the late 1980s helped broaden comics' appeal which would allow titles like *The Sandman* and *The Invisibles* to see publication from mainstream comics publishers, a number of other factors came to a head, including the ever thorny questions of creator's rights and censorship. The creation of Image Comics by seven artists who had grown popular drawing the likes of Spider-Man and the New Mutants at Marvel generated great excitement in the fan community and the early Image Comics releases sold in phenomenal quantities; back issues by these "hot" artists began to leap in price and the comics-as-investments boom of the early 1990s was born, fuelled by an influx of speculative dealers who had previously dealt in baseball cards (and whose markets were hit badly by National Baseball League labour strikes in the early 1990s). The trading card philosophy was applied to comics, creating deliberate collectables by limiting supply, offering variant covers and using gimmicks like holographic covers. The arrival of magazines supporting the speculative craze helped talk up demand and it was not uncommon to see comics only two or three months old selling for more than ten times their cover price as the supplies dried up. Some of Moore's early *Swamp Thing*s were going at one point for twenty or twenty-five pounds – not a bad return on a cover price of twenty-five or thirty pence.

With buyers willing to spend that much on a single issue, publishers could easily justify bringing out "prestige" titles and hardbacks with fully-painted art. Only five years earlier only the crème de la crème got this treatment (*Dark Knight Returns* and *The Killing Joke* among them), but before long one or two "prestige" titles were coming out every week. To generate publicity DC killed their most popular character in *Superman* issue 75 (1993), gaining national coverage and a sale of over 7 million copies; when that furore died down, they broke the Batman's back as part of the 'Knightfall' storyline (1994). Superman returned shortly after. Batman got better.

The boom lasted a scant few years and was a short-term strategy at best – how could a comic with a 7 million printrun become scarce? – and one that did nothing to move the medium forward. The contrast with that approach and Moore's literary ambitions at the time could hardly be greater.

This was also a time of personal problems for Moore: he and Phyllis divorced (and she went off with Deborah Delano). Among the consequences of that was the end of Mad Love; and Moore lost a great deal of the money he'd earned during the comics boom.

Some of Moore's projects didn't see the light of day at all. He was to write for a Fantagraphics anthology series, and had written a couple of scripts. He'd also devised a science fiction series with John Totleben, 'Lux Brevis' (recently printed in *Kimota!*, a history of *Miracleman* by George Khoury).

By now, Moore's creative ambitions stretched further than comics. His fortieth birthday in 1993 seems to have marked a turning point, when he consciously set out to explore new creative areas. He became interested in the occult, and became a performance artist.

He also started to write *Voice Of The Fire*, published in 1996, a collection of short stories set in Northampton, which builds up into a larger narrative. Moore's home town is often used by market researchers because it represents in microcosm the average British population. As Moore says, today its main employers are the Barclaycard credit control offices and the Carlsberg brewery, the best symbols of contemporary values you could wish for. In the book, Moore uses incidents suggested by local history to extrapolate the story of Britain and its people, particularly how imagination and 'visions' have shaped us. It's a mistake to start the book with a long story told from the viewpoint of a caveman with a vocabulary of a few hundred words – Moore himself admits that "while it's probably not the best commercial move, you could argue it's not a mistake but a deliberately non-commercial stance" – but once that's out of the way, the book is poetic and evocative. Like *From Hell* and *Watchmen*, a world is conjured up from patterns and recurring themes.

And then, perhaps most surprisingly of all, Alan Moore returned to writing superhero comics.

5. The Return

Image

Some fans were horrified when Moore started to write for Image, a company reviled by some sections of fandom for shallow stories and unsubtle characters. It was a company that had recently been formed by a partnership of seven artists (Todd McFarlane, Jim Lee, Rob Liefeld, Jim Valentino, Marc Silvestri, Erik Larsen and Whilce Portacio, who quickly left), who released titles from their studios under the Image banner, retaining complete control over their properties but at the same time benefiting from being part of a brand name comics company. At a time when the comics literati were being wowed by *The Sandman* and Moore's work in *Taboo*, Image traded on 'bad girl' art (women with large chests and bottoms, one or the other always sticking out) and graphic violence. Image quickly earned a reputation for a crude house art style – all snarling faces, speed lines, and sloppy composition. Moore's first published work for Image was *Spawn* 8, which had a cover date of March 1993, making it his first new superhero work since *The Killing Joke*, published almost exactly five years before.

Moore has never explained his motives for choosing Image for his return to the comics mainstream, but a couple of reasons are obvious. He'd fallen out with DC and, before that, he'd vowed never to work for Marvel again. There were other companies around – Dark Horse, for example, were publishing Frank Miller's *Sin City* (and had published the American edition of *A Small Killing*). But Image was a new company that had quickly established itself, and within a couple of years – incredibly in such a conservative and beleaguered market – *Spawn*, created by Todd McFarlane, had become one of the best-selling comics. But perhaps it was the management behind Image that Moore found most attractive. Image was a creator-owned imprint, as such it seemed more in tune with creators' concerns, such as subsidiary rights, the return of original artwork and royalty rates. DC and Marvel were part of big corporations, and above all else they were always going to resist radical reinterpretations of characters like Superman and Spiderman. McFarlane, for his part, seems to have recognised that his titles were short of writing talent, and when Moore agreed to doing a guest spot, others – Neil Gaiman, Dave Sim and Frank Miller – soon followed.

Moore stuck with Image, apparently getting on well with most, if not all, of the six partners. Jim Valentino backed a Moore mini-series, *1963*. It's an inventive series, mixing dynamic stories with some good-natured jokes at the expense of comics. The series was a pastiche of Jack Kirby stories drawn for Marvel in the sixties, with their rather overblown style, colourful characters and cosmic scale. The running theme of the series is that 1963 was a more innocent time, but not an idyll – there is still the Cold War, this is just before the big civil rights movements. It was seen by many critics as a retrograde step from the writer of *From Hell*. A few years down the line, though, it became clear Moore was actually a little ahead of the curve. He wasn't the only person doing Kirby pastiches (In *Doom Patrol* 53, a year before, Grant Morrison had imagined the "realistic" Vertigo characters like John Constantine as colourful Kirby-style heroes), and the pendulum was starting to swing back to allow the return of the more kitsch and camp elements into superhero stories. Writers and readers were starting to realise that whatever real-world elements were introduced, superheroes would never be all that "realistic." Comics like *Flex Mentallo*, *Astro City* and *Powers* have come along stressing how different a world with superheroes would be, rather than trying to imagine how they would operate in ours. Superhero comics have come to embrace the absurdities of their own internal logic, rather than trying to rationalise them. Superheroes are allowed to be entertaining, uplifting and heroic, rather than "dark" and "gritty." *1963* was to be capped off with a *1963 Annual*, where the 1963 characters met the regular Image ones, but this was delayed, then became a victim of disputes between the partners at Image.

Spawn

Moore wrote four Spawn mini-series in quick succession – two which followed Spawn's arch-enemy, the demonic clown Violator (the three-part *Violator*, the four part *Violator/Badrock*). He concentrated on Spawn himself in *Spawn: Blood Feud*, where Spawn is suspected of a series of bloody murders which have been committed by the powerful vampire Heartless John. In interviews, Moore stated that he was writing "better than average stories for 13 to 15-year-olds." In those terms, the series work well – they are well-told adventure tales, with some interesting twists and narrative tricks. Initial suspicions that Moore's writing would seem very odd coupled with artists working to the Image house style were unfounded – if anything, it's disconcerting how effortlessly Moore fits in, and how exuberant he seems. What he (along with Neil Gaiman) managed to do was to start realising some of the potential of the Spawn character. Between them, Moore and Gaiman developed the cosmology of the Spawn universe. Moore's first issue, and some of his subsequent ones, explored Hell (a similar Hell to that envisaged in *Swamp Thing*). Spawn had been a supernatural crime fighter … now a larger purpose was revealed. In the end, though, even a good *Spawn* story isn't very substantial, and there was a very strong sense that Moore was slumming it.

WildC.A.T.S.

In 1995, Moore became the writer of *WildC.A.T.S.* with issue 21, only his second regular monthly American comic. His run would last fourteen issues (plus a brief reprise in issue 50). It was an odd book, created by Jim Lee and his Wildstorm studio, a superteam split between "street level" characters and those caught up in an eternal galactic war. Unlike most of his revamps, Moore didn't contrive to blow up the universe or reconstruct his heroes from the ground up; instead he split the action between a gang war on Earth and the alien characters returning to their home planet. There aren't many parallels between the two stories, so the book has a somewhat disjointed, schizophrenic feel. There are some nice ideas, characters and jokes, but the series never quite gels, because it's essentially two different half-length stories every month, a situation aggravated by what feels like a different art team in every issue – the artist is important to the feel of a book, and regular artists here would help give a sense of continuity to the characters and events. It's no coincidence that the best issues are those that feature the work of penciller Travis Charest, who did Moore's first issue and subsequently managed a continuous run of seven issues. When a crossover event, *Fire In Heaven*, imposes itself halfway through Moore's run, more momentum is lost. *WildC.A.T.S.* under Moore is a good team book, an entertaining read, but somehow you feel Moore should be better than this. It's not special.

In early 1996, Moore wrote a four-part series that teamed up Spawn and WildC.A.T.S., who travel to a future where Spawn has taken control of the United States.

Moore was now telling interviewers that comics could be used to explore important issues, but superhero comics that tried were inevitably rather crass. There was a place for superheroes, he said, telling uplifting fantasy stories, inspiring hope and using them as role models. With his early Image work, there's a real sense that Moore is steering away from "realistic" issues. In the process, though, there's inevitably something unsatisfying about the stories. You don't feel that Moore's heart is in it, there's none of the obsession with detail you see in most of his work.

Supreme

Far more successful was Moore's work on *Supreme*. *Supreme* had been one of the more misconceived books in the Image range. It had been created by Rob Liefeld and was essentially a dumb power fantasy, with a Superman-type hero killing his enemies, having ever more cosmic adventures and lacking any of the charm or character that had made Superman a success in the first place. Moore revamped the title, using his by now rather familiar tactic of wiping out what had gone before, giving the hero amnesia and revealing that everything we'd learned to that point was a lie. But this time, instead of scraping away whimsy in favour of realism, Moore did just the opposite. Supreme quickly becomes the silver age Superman in all but name, complete with his very own Supergirl (Suprema), Superdog (Radar), Lois Lane (Judy Jordan), Lex Luthor (Darius Dax) and even Kryptonite (Supremium). The issues almost always contain a flashback that's a homage to silver or golden age comics. The original plan was that Curt Swan, the definitive artist for Superman in the sixties and seventies, would handle the flashback sequences but sadly he died just before he was due to start.

There is, of course, more to what Moore is doing than lovingly recreating some pretty cheesy sixties comics. They work perfectly on that straightforward level, but also as an ironic, knowing take on the history of comics and the plight of their protagonists. Supreme is the oldest superhero, an invulnerable, flying icon who has been around since the thirties and seen the nature of his adventures change over the years. Supreme's alter ego, Ethan Crane, is a comic book artist, drawing the Superman-like rip-off character Omniman. He has to deal with the whims of his publisher and his ridiculous British writer, who has plans for an elaborate "superdog rape" story. A lesser writer than Moore might have used this as a vehicle to mock the early stories, or to hark back to simpler times, or to lay into the "dark" characters of the eighties. In his first issue Moore hits an inclusionist note – Supreme discovers that all the various versions of Supreme go to a limbo dimension, the Supremacy, when they die (or their series is cancelled). Every story 'exists,' none is more valid than another. Moore is concerned with the power of the original stories: the mythic simplicity, the compelling surrealism, as well as the underlying notes of kinkiness or their simplifications of complex issues. The art in the issues is split between the Image present-day house style and silver age-style flashbacks (usually by Rick Veitch) which reflect ironically or tellingly on those present-day events. It's a simple, but effective way of making a point, and if there are problems, it's that the flashback stories are almost too familiar – the flashback in issue 43 is almost a straight remake of 'The Super-Key To Fort Superman' in *Action Comics* 241 and that the novelty is in danger of wearing off within a few issues.

Just as it was beginning to feel a little formulaic, *Supreme* got a jolt in the arm from the arrival of a new, regular artist Chris Sprouse in issue 50. That issue is perhaps the standout issue of the run. In 'A Love Supreme,' Ethan and Diana meet up to discuss a possible romance for Omniman. Their scenes are just the two of them in Diana's apartment. Diana quickly decides that a relationship with an ordinary woman and Omniman's secret identity would be too dull – "all you'd have is pages of people in ordinary clothing sitting around talking," she declares. Of course that's exactly what this issue of *Supreme* is, and naturally, as it's Moore writing, these scenes manage to generate some real romantic tension using slight hesitations, body language or one of the two accidentally making a suggestive remark. Moore has his cake and eats it. Intercut with this very human drama is 'The Many Loves Of Supreme,' a series of lurid imaginary stories in which we see Supreme marry, variously but always disastrously, his human love interest Judy Jordan, angel Luriel, and Glory (that's Lois Lane, Lori Lemaris and Wonder Woman, for those of you who speak Superman). The flashbacks are entertaining pastiches of similar Superman stories that are almost beyond parody. In one original *Superman* story from 1963, Superman can't decide between childhood sweetheart Lana Lang and the great love of his adult life, Lois Lane and so splits himself in two and has both! Of course, it's the commentary on the old *Supreme* stories from Ethan and Diana ("God, that attitude is so fifties"), and the will-they-won't-they of their relationship that's the real source of interest. In the end, Diana is on the verge of committing herself to writing a relationship between Omniman and Linda Lake, but talks herself out of it … and inadvertently stops Ethan declaring his love for her. In one issue, Moore combines superhero action, comedy, an ironic spin on comics' history and iconography, great art, a clever script, intricate plotting, a vivid contrast drawn between the way things work in comics and in real life, and a touching human story at the heart of it all.

Supreme works best when it's in icon territory. Superman and Batman, Clark and Lois, Superboy and Lex Luthor, Supergirl and Wonder Woman.

Anyone who knows the characters knows the basics and the powerful underlying narratives, like the Superman-Lois-Clark love triangle, which have fuelled hundreds of stories over the years, and are familiar from films and TV as well as comics. The series goes off the rails a little when dealing with the minutiae of comics, the stuff that requires specialist knowledge. Most of the people reading *Supreme: The Return* 6 would probably recognise that it is a pastiche of Jack Kirby's work, but Moore doesn't wring any archetypal power from it. For once, he doesn't find the human-level story.

Supreme was Moore's first big sales and critical success for a fair few years. By his fourth issue, *Supreme* had won an Overstreet Fan Award, and the first two issues were quickly reprinted. Suddenly, Moore was back.

Awesome

Image, though, were having problems. Rob Liefeld had started to publish some titles (including *Supreme*) under his Maximum Press banner, bypassing Image. The other partners gradually became concerned by this and Marc Silvestri left citing "differences" with the other partners. Within the space of a few months, Liefeld had left Image (and Silvestri returned almost as soon as that happened). Out on his own, Liefeld changed the name of Maximum Press to Awesome Entertainment and gave Moore the task of reinventing the whole universe in which the *Supreme* stories were set, now designated "the Awesome Universe."

Moore must have appreciated the irony – with Swamp Thing, Marvelman and Superman, he'd taken fifteen, twenty, thirty, even fifty-year-old characters and reinterpreted them for a modern audience. Moore found himself revamping characters like Glory and Youngblood that had barely been around two years. His solution was breathtaking and cocky – he created a long and distinguished history for these new characters, retro-fitting a fake silver and golden age for them. It was a perfect solution – it gave the characters firm roots and enriched the shared universe of the characters.

The fact that *Glory* was a rip-off of *Wonder Woman* suddenly became the title's great strength, rather than its great weakness: it could evoke the original when it wanted to, but the sixty-year history wouldn't be a millstone around it. Awesome would eventually publish Moore's notes as the *Awesome Universe Handbook*, and in that we get to see his reasoning. This could be Wonder Woman done properly, a chance to "go back to the 'parent' character ... and try to analyse all the elements – even the unlikely or absurd ones – that make the initial character tick in the first place." Wonder Woman was brought up on a woman-only island, having a lasso that gave her power over men she encircled and wristbands that symbolised women's historical subservience. She had a parade of female villains who, as Moore hardly needed to point out, wore Nazi uniforms and catsuits they could have bought off the peg at any fetishwear shop. The creators of Wonder Woman had long steered away from any hint of sex, just as the creators of Batman had tried to eradicate even the possibility that Batman and Robin's relationship was anything other than wholesome. Moore was quick to stress "I don't think we should ever state that the Isle of Thule [Glory's home] is a lesbian pornotopia, but I don't think we should ever state that it isn't, either." This knowing, "don't ask, don't tell" policy allowed everything from the most innocent interpretation to the filthiest imaginable.

The plan was that Moore would write *Glory* and the teen team comic *Youngblood*, as well as continuing with *Supreme*. He kicked off in the three-part *Judgment Day*, which sketched in the new history of the Awesome Universe, using a variety of artists from all eras of comics history, and a storyline revolving around a trial that contrived to bring just about every superhero there was into the courtroom to give evidence in a series of short flashback homage sequences. If Moore's *Supreme* had been a cheeky borrowing of Superman's heritage, this was an all-out raid on the whole of comics history. The series is entertaining in itself; as a pilot, it opens a new door.

Moore had big plans. He wanted Simon Bisley to draw a series called *The League Of Extraordinary Gentlefolk*, which would team up all the great heroes of Victorian melodrama. He'd also find time to write a twelve-part mini-series, *Warchild*, and at least kick off the series *The Allies*, the big 'grown up' team book, equivalent to the JLA or the Avengers, with the headline heroes and heroines of the Awesome Universe all grouped together in one book. But it was not to be. Away from the relative security of Image, Awesome ran into trouble. Just as the range was cohering artistically, and Moore was on the verge of writing what amounted to a comic a week, the money started to run out. As the release schedule started slipping, cash flow became more erratic, making the schedule even less reliable. *Supreme* abruptly vanished, the promised *Glory* series was constantly on the verge of publication, but never made it to the shops. *Youngblood*'s own title came and went, a new issue appearing a year later without warning under the title *Awesome Adventures*. One sign of desperation was the appearance, in isolation, of Moore's notes for Glory and Youngblood in *Alan Moore's Awesome Handbook*. Supreme reappeared after a year, as *Supreme: The Return*, and carried on, erratically, for another year, but it eventually fizzled out just before the run reached Moore's final two issues.

It's a real shame. The three issues of *Youngblood* that made it out are lovely – a clever team book, with just the right mix of characterisation, comedy, ludicrous flights of fancy and colourful action, with art by Steve Skroce and Lary Stucker. The one issue of *Glory* that surfaced was a 'zero' issue, one sold at conventions as a taster of what's to come, rather than one that's part of the series itself. As such, it's a fairly disposable prelude. But even here, the basic set-up that Moore establishes looks intriguing. Both these titles are instantly accessible, but with enough depth to reward close attention and rereading, just as comics should be.

America's Best Comics

Salvation was at hand. Moore had stayed on good terms with the other Image partners, particularly Jim Lee, head of Wildstorm, the Image studio that produced *WildC.A.T.S.*. Lee offered Moore his own imprint. Moore settled on the name America's Best Comics, ABC for short, and quickly signed up to write what was renamed *The League Of Extraordinary Gentlemen*, which would now be drawn by *2000AD* stalwart Kevin O'Neill. Before this appeared, there was one last surprise – Lee visited Moore and told him he was going to sell Wildstorm (and with it ABC) to DC Comics. Moore found himself back with a company he'd vowed never to work with again. With artists, colourists and letterers already committed to the new line, Moore decided that too many people were involved for him to pull out and with firm reassurances that he would not have to deal directly with DC executives and that his work would not be interfered with, ABC was launched in early 1999.

The League Of Extraordinary Gentlemen

The League Of Extraordinary Gentlemen takes a standard of the superhero genre, the 'team-up book,' and applies it to the great heroes of Victorian fiction. The British government of 1898 assemble a group of adventurers – Allan Quatermain, Captain Nemo, Dr Jekyll, The Invisible Man and Mina Harker (from *Dracula*) to fight for Queen and country. In a counterpoint to the London of *From Hell*, this is a collage of the Victorian London of the imagination – a place where every character who's named (and a fair few that aren't) come from fiction, so there are characters from Sherlock Holmes, Jules Verne, HG Wells, Bram Stoker, Victorian erotica, even the ancestors of the *EastEnders* (who work for an ancient Artful Dodger). Our heroes battle Fu Manchu and Moriarty in a world that's a heightened version of the real Victorian era – one where British engineers are building a Channel Bridge, and (in a nod to *From Hell*) British secret service agents wear Masonic insignia on their uniforms.

It's exuberant, accessible, earthy, colourful, funny … perhaps a little lightweight compared with Moore's classics like *Watchmen* and *V For Vendetta*, but it's a comic you can pick up and read even if you aren't a comics fan. The story has twists and turns and red herrings – and a surprise villain whose identity is actually a shock, even though it's blindingly obvious in retrospect.

Demand for the first issue, which was released in early 1999, took everyone by surprise. The comics market had been flat for a number of years, the heady days when first issues shot up in value within a few months seemed long gone. *League* changed that. As people read it, word of mouth spread and it started selling out. The second issue vanished from shops a month later. At this point, it became apparent that Kevin O'Neill was having problems keeping to the schedule. To their credit DC/Wildstorm took a situation that might, as Moore knew all too well, have killed the sales and critical momentum, and turned it to their advantage. They quickly reissued the material from issues 1 and 2 in a Bumper Compendium, allowing all those who'd missed the title to catch up. By now, the original editions of the first and second issues were fetching five or six times cover price. The other ABC titles were starting to appear, and retailers were encouraged to look at the success of *League* when they preordered them. When the third issue appeared, even with a larger print run and retailers anticipating high demand, it sold out. It would be several months before the fourth issue, which again sold well and earned a second Bumper Compendium. The fifth issue was delayed for seven months … and the first printing was pulped for legal reasons, delaying it by another week. By now, the delays were the subject of jokes in the letters column: when asked if O'Neill was selling the original artwork, the editor replied "Mr Sorenson, we are not entirely convinced that Mr O'Neill is currently even *drawing* original artwork for the series, let alone selling it." It did nothing to dampen anticipation for new issues. As the sixth issue appeared, a hardback collection of the whole series was announced.

A sequel is planned and, in one interview, Moore has suggested that it's going to be partly set on Mars and feature a war between the Martians of Wells, Burroughs and CS Lewis. Having learned their lesson, Wildstorm are waiting for Kevin O'Neill to finish the artwork before announcing a release date (itself only possible because of DC's relative financial strength – smaller companies would have to release early instalments to pay for the later ones). The first series has been optioned as a film by Don Murphy and Jane Hamsher.

The America's Best Comics line proper started a couple of months after *The League Of Extraordinary Gentlemen*'s first issue. The original plan was that there would be four titles a month, or one a week. It has not worked out like that in practice, but the slippage has not been as bad as Moore's fans became used to in the Nineties. Those four titles would represent a spread of styles, but would all be released in standard American comic book format. They are *Tom Strong*, *Promethea*, *Top Ten* and an anthology series, *Tomorrow Stories*.

Tom Strong

Tom Strong seems to go out of its way to invite comparisons with *Supreme*. Tom Strong himself is another long-lived Superman type, albeit one closer to the original Superman – a man who could only "leap tall buildings with a single bound" and was "faster than a speeding bullet" … not like the modern Superman or Supreme, who can juggle planets while flying faster than the speed of light. Tom Strong is also a long-lived, straightforward hero. Like *Supreme*, each issue is structured with a flashback scene harking back to Tom Strong's old days. And, if that wasn't already enough, it's even drawn by Moore's *Supreme* collaborators, Chris Sprouse and Al Gordon. But there are some major differences. Moore is indeed telling Superman stories that take the character back to basics, as he had with Marvelman and Supreme (and Superman himself, of course). But here he goes a little further back – Tom Strong has got more in common with the pulp heroes from the mid-Thirties like Solomon Kane and (most particularly) Doc Savage. He's a 'superman' in the eugenic sense, rather than a superhero.

Tom Strong is a simple comic. The stories are straightforward, Sprouse's art is all clean lines and wide open spaces – there's little in the way of clutter. This most definitely doesn't mean it's easy to write – just the opposite: if it puts a foot wrong, there's nothing to hide behind. It's a more subtle comic than *Supreme*. The post-ironic feel is still there, but

Tom Strong doesn't wear it on its sleeve. It's not perfect. Some of *Supreme*'s best moments come when the fantastic and mundane worlds meet, and there's little opportunity for that in *Tom Strong* – while Tom Strong has a family, they are a family of superheroes, talking gorillas and robots. Another problem is that while *Tom Strong* was sold as going back to basics with the superman archetype, paring everything back and effectively starting again, Moore found it difficult to resist pastiching comics history. In *Supreme* and *Watchmen* it fits in perfectly ... here it seems to muddle the message. This world might have 'science heroes,' but they act remarkably like superheroes would.

That said, it is ABC's most accessible comic, and Tom Strong is an appealing, refreshing character.

Top Ten

Top Ten is a change of pace. It's set in Neopolis, a city where everyone has superpowers. It's the story of the people who have to police such a place, and it's a *Hill Street Blues*-style ensemble piece, with a bewildering range of characters. As is often the way, other people had the same idea around the same time. *Top Ten* is joined on the shelf by Brian Michael Bendis' *Powers* and Kurt Busiek's *Astro City*, and has coincided with Greg Rucka, a crime novelist, shifting the focus of the Batman stories in *Detective Comics* towards the Gotham Police Department. Meanwhile, the TV series *The Sopranos* is having an influence on comics, with titles like *Daredevil* and *Batman: Dark Victory* concentrating on fighting the mob. A year or so earlier, *Top Ten* would have been unique, now it's just one of a lot of "cops and capes" series. Rucka and Bendis, relative newcomers, are also extremely talented writers – *Powers* in particular has a claim on being the best new comic for quite some time (and is clearly influenced by *Watchmen*).

That said, there's no denying that *Top Ten* is good stuff. The sheer richness of each and every panel means that it needs to be read three or four times to spot everything. Each page is packed with visual jokes (a poster for the film *Businessman* promises its superhuman audience "You'll believe a man can't fly"), visual puns, nods to comics history and cameo appearances from pop cultural icons from the Daleks to Wallace and Gromit. A lesser writer would concentrate on that at the expense of story, but each issue gives a couple of self-contained detective stories, develops some bigger cases, moves on a few long-running stories and foreshadows future developments. Not only that, Moore manages to give us a large cast of regulars, held together in a complex web of relationships. It's almost certainly the most densely-packed regular comic there's ever been. And – a mark of a truly great writer – other people could get a whole issue out of some of the gags and ideas Moore comes up with and disposes of in a single panel.

Tomorrow Stories

The most experimental of the ABC line is the anthology series, *Tomorrow Stories*. While British comics have remained anthologies filled with lots of short strips throughout their history, the format is unusual in America nowadays. *Tomorrow Stories* has four running strips and they tend to be comedic, or at least a little arch.

Greyshirt is a crime fighter in the mould of The Spirit or The Question. Drawn by Rick Veitch, the series has been used by Moore to tell lurid, pulpy crime stories, using experimental layouts and narratives.

Cobweb is another crime fighter, a decadent woman, as sensuous as Melinda Gebbie can make her. More pulp fiction, this time with kinkiness and eroticism that's so near the surface it could barely be called a subtext.

The First American is a complete change of pace – a satirical superhero strip, whose most obvious antecedents are *MAD Comics* and the Simon & Kirby strip *The Fighting American*. The square-jawed, vain hero and his barely legal girl sidekick face off against the forces of commercialism and popular prejudice, representing the crass, greedy America that icons of the American way of life like Superman and Captain America never seem to encounter.

For the first issues, the fourth strip was Jack B Quick, about a young boy genius whose experiments lead to *Alice In Wonderland*-like logical absurdity. He butters a cat's feet to create perpetual motion – because the cat spins forever, trying both to land on its feet and buttered side up. Twenty years ago, in *2000AD*, Moore was writing light-hearted Dr Dibworthy and Abelard Snazz strips about geniuses who invariably end up destroying everything in the pursuit of science.

Jack B Quick was popular but, to give Kevin Nowlan enough time to draw the strip, for the moment he was replaced by Splash Brannigan, a strip of energetic visual comedy almost in the Chuck Jones mould.

Promethea

If Tom Strong sounded like Supreme, when *Promethea* was announced it sounded for all the world like Moore was creating another Wonder Woman clone, like Glory. The obvious suspicion was that he'd found a way of getting his *Glory* scripts made, and it would be little more than reheated leftovers. In the event, though, *Promethea* is nothing of the sort. Moore has taken the mythical type of superhero – Wonder Woman (the daughter of the Queen of the Amazons of Greek legend) or Thor (Marvel's take on Norse mythology) – and created a series about magic, myth and the power of story. What looked like a poor man's *Wonder Woman* has ended up as *The Sandman* for grown-ups instead of arrested adolescents.

Sophie Bangs, an ordinary teenage girl living in a hyper-real New York, accidentally becomes the latest in a long line of Prometheas. Promethea is a fictional character, a powerful woman who's been written about for centuries, and who has come to have a real, physical existence. Sophie/Promethea is learning the extent of her powers, her place in the universe, and is also managing to fit in some traditional superheroic action. The series tackles some pretty big and important themes – the power of imagination, the nature of fiction, representation of gender, cosmology, the occult. But it's far more even than that. At the same time, Moore is also using some interesting tricks with the medium – JH Williams III and Mick Gray design each page with complex running motifs, intricately detailed page borders, experiments with computer-generated imagery and the like. Moore has always been a writer worth following for the incidental details in his books. *Promethea* creates a vibrant, complex New York that, in story terms, is little more than a backdrop for Sophie's journey of self-exploration. Special mention needs to be made of Weeping Gorilla, a cartoon character who appears on billboards in the background of some of the scenes set in the city. Weeping Gorilla is a throwaway detail, literally just there to fill space, but Moore has created a hilarious single-panel cartoon, a sensitive gorilla, whose angst-ridden proclamations (such as "Forty's just a number, after all," "Maybe we expect too much of George Lucas") are at least as funny as 'real' newspaper cartoons.

Promethea works best when a block of issues are read in one go – reading the collected edition, the story flows noticeably more smoothly, you don't forget the incidental developments while waiting for the next instalment. The first year's worth of issues barely covers Sophie's first couple of days as Promethea, so at monthly intervals, it does feel a little slow. But there's a real sense with *Promethea*, missing from a lot of Moore's work with Image and Awesome, that he cares about *Promethea*, that he's making a personal statement. Here, the pastiches of comics history build up into a belief system, a personal cosmology. Moore has often dealt with the physical reality of ideas, in stories as diverse as *V For Vendetta* and *Supreme*. Here, he writes a series specifically on the subject.

Moore freely admits that he doesn't have a masterplan for the ABC range, but all the books are steady sellers. He's planning an SF series *Comet Rangers*, and is bringing Steve Moore in to help write *Tom Strong* stories (in a new anthology series *Tom Strong's Terrific Tales*). *Greyshirt* has his own mini-series (written by Rick Veitch), and *Smax The Barbarian* and *The 49ers* will explore the history of *Top Ten*'s Neopolis. Moore will continue to write many of the titles, but wants to create an environment where other writers and artists can use his creations to tell good stories.

Nothing Ever Ends

Today, Moore has his own range of comics, one underwritten by AOL Time Warner. He gets the artists he wants to use – long-term friends like Rick Veitch and Melinda Gebbie, people he's known as long as he's been working in comics, like Jim Baikie and Steve Moore, as well as "hot" artists like Alex Ross. Each of the ABC strips has a distinctive look, and they are probably the most beautifully crafted comics out today. They come out roughly every month, but only when they are ready – there aren't filler issues by understudy artists, or ones that have been rushed. As soon as there's enough material, the stories are collected in beautiful hardback editions, which in time become mass-market paperbacks.

They aren't perfect. It's easy to understand why some people have criticised the ABC titles for a lack of ambition. With an unprecedented degree of security, couldn't Moore take greater risks, experiment a bit more, steer away from superheroes? Writing four titles a month is all-consuming – Moore doesn't have time to write short stories for the independent sector at the moment, or to write his second novel (which he's told interviewers is called *A Grammar*). There's some experimentation being snuck in under the wire in *Promethea* and *Tomorrow Stories*, and all five ABC titles to date have been good stuff, but nothing like the mould-breaking work he attempted with *Big Numbers* or *From Hell*. Sales across the board have been solid, around thirty to forty thousand; profitable, but not spectacular. Moore's answer to those critics is simple – small press books like *From Hell* sold less than half that, when issues actually came out. Now he is consciously working within the mainstream, to help raise the standards of comics that people actually read. Coincidence or not, his re-emergence has come at a time of renaissance in the comics industry. In Britain a new owner and editor are reinvigorating *2000AD*. A new chief executive at Marvel has given the company a shot in the arm, with titles like Grant Morrison's *New X-Men*. At DC, film director Kevin Smith has made *Green Arrow* a sales sensation. Oni Press, a new small-press imprint for non-superhero titles can seemingly do no wrong. Frank Miller and Bryan Talbot have created sequels to their masterworks.

As he approaches his fiftieth birthday, Moore has, finally, managed to find creative freedom and financial security, as well as artistic integrity, in a growing market. He's writing superhero books, but – despite a few skirmishes – on his terms. Working for America's Best Comics, he doesn't have to worry about a lack of respect or resources, the obstacles that have held him back in the past. Away from the world of comics, he seems more confident. He's a performance artist, a magician, a novelist. He's living with Melinda Gebbie. His daughter studies *V For Vendetta* as part of a graphic novel component of her English degree. The film version of *From Hell* has just hit Number One at the US Box Office

Moore has consistently been the best comics writer in the field. He's almost always been ahead of the game, he's very rarely, artistically at least, got things wrong. There's the palpable sense that he's gearing up to produce something special. There's no doubt we've not seen his last masterpiece. But we're used to masterpieces from him, now. We were promised a revolution – and if anyone's going to deliver it, it's going to be Alan Moore.

6. Bibliography

Comics

The list below is not a checklist of individual comics. It groups the material together by story or character, and sets out how it has been presented over the years. Some of Moore's work is readily available, in a variety of formats, some is practically impossible to find.

So what's a reader to do?

It is possible to walk into any good bookshop and buy something by Alan Moore – work like *Watchmen, The Killing Joke, From Hell* and *V For Vendetta* has been collected into paperback editions, some of which have been in print for fifteen years. His current America's Best Comics work is being collected into lavish hardback editions, which are easy to track down.

Comic shops and marts, of course, are good places to look, and a lot of his work from the eighties can be found in back issue boxes, often at far lower prices than they commanded at the height of the comics boom.

There was a time during that boom when just about everything Moore had written in Britain was reprinted for the American market, often in the form of an American comic book – a process that involved shrinking and resizing art to fit the smaller, proportionately taller, pages and (often rather hurriedly) colouring the black and white pictures. While this is not always to the material's advantage, American comics have always tended to survive better than their British counterparts, so this is often the only place collectors have any realistic chance of finding early material by Moore.

Generally, the more disposable the original, the more people disposed of it, and the harder it is to find. Anyone looking to find a complete run of the *Northants Post* for the *Maxwell The Magic Cat* strips is going to be looking for a long while. Even finding Moore's early British superhero work can be quite tricky. At the other end of the scale, items like the *Watchmen* and *Miracleman* hardbacks were expensive, and produced in tiny numbers (often only hundreds). Common sense says that the older or less commercial something is, on the whole, the harder it will be to find.

Even more so than most items, comics are only worth what people are willing to pay for them, and there can be huge variations in that. In that spirit, I've not attempted to put a price on anything, and have only noted where an item is particularly rare or sought-after.

A.B.C. (America's Best Comics)

An eight-page strip previewing the ABC Comics line appeared as a *Wizard Preview* (March 1999, art: Chris Sprouse/Al Gordon), which also included sketchbook material.

The League Of Extraordinary Gentlemen (art: Kevin O'Neill) was a six-part mini-series with an erratic publishing history. The first part came out in March 1999, making it the first comic under the ABC imprint. The second followed in April. These were reprinted (minus the prose story *Allan And The Sundered Veil*) in a Bumper Compendium in May. Issue 3 appeared in June, issue 4 in November. Again, these sold out and were reprinted in the Bumper Compendium II (again without the prose story). Issue 5 eventually appeared in June 2000, and the first print run was immediately withdrawn and pulped (an advert appeared for a 'Marvel Vagina Syringe,' which the publishers felt could be seen as an insult to rival Marvel Comics – some of these issues had already been sent out to reviewers, and are now worth a small fortune), but a reissue (still labelled 'First Printing,' but with the vaginal syringe now made by 'Amaze') appeared almost immediately. Issue 6 appeared in September 2000. The series was quickly collected into the hardback *The League Of Extraordinary Gentlemen* (December 2000), which also reprints the *League* game from the ABC 64-page giant. The sequel series is scheduled for 2002.

Tom Strong Issue 1 (art: Chris Sprouse/Al Gordon) appeared in June 1999. Issue 4 was the first with a short story by a guest artist (Arthur Adams), subsequent issues have the same by Jerry Ordway, Dave Gibbons, Gary Frank, Alan Weiss, Paul Chadwick, Gary Gianni, Kyle Baker, Russ Heath, Pete Poplaski and Hilary Barta. There is a new anthology series of Tom Strong stories, half written by Alan Moore, half by Steve Moore: *Tom Strong's Terrific Tales* (January 2002, the first issue has two stories by Alan Moore, with art by Paul Rivoche and Jamie Hernandez).

Promethea Issue 1 (art: J H Williams III/Mick Gray) was published in August 1999.

Top 10 Issue 1 (art: Gene Ha & Zander Cannon) was published in September 1999. The 'first season' concluded with issue 12 (October 2001). 2002 will see two spin-offs: the mini-series *Smax The Barbarian* (art: Zander Cannon), and the graphic novel *The 49ers* (art: Gene Ha).

Tomorrow Stories Issue 1 (October 1999) kicks off with four regular six-page strips: Cobweb (art: Melinda Gebbie), Greyshirt (art: Rick Veitch), Jack B Quick (art: Kevin Nowlan), The First American (art: Jim Baikie). There is no Jack B Quick in Issue 5, from Issue 6 (March 2000) its place has been taken by Splash Brannigan (art: Hilary Barta), but he returns for one issue in 10 (June 2001). Issues 9 and 10 (February 2001, June 2001) sees Cobweb drawn by Dame Darcy, issue 11 (October 2001) by Joyce Chin.

The *America's Best Comics 64-Page Giant* has stories featuring the ABC regular characters by their usual artists (including a *The League Of Extraordinary Gentlemen* board game). The Splash Brannigan strip is drawn by Kyle Baker, The First American by Sergio Aragones. The Tom Strong (art: Humberto Ramos & John Totleben) and Promethea (art: Eric Shanower) stories are by Steve Moore (although the Tom Strong tale is credited to Alan Moore on the contents page). The eight-page strip from the *Wizard Preview* is reprinted here.

The regular ABC titles are being collected in hardback editions, each collecting six or seven issues at a time, with a trade paperback due to follow after several months. It appears that *Tomorrow Stories* will be collected by individual strip, and so it will be a while before enough material is available to reprint.

Alan Moore's Songbook

Negative Burn published a number of lyrics to songs Moore originally wrote for his band The Emperors of Ice Cream in the early Nineties, which they set to images:

'Another Suburban Romance,' (Issue 9, March 1994, art: Ken Meyer Jr)

'London' (Issue 10, April 1994, art: Richard Case)

'Positively Bridge Street' (Issue 11, May 1994, art: Phillip Hester)

'14.2.99' (Issue 12, June 1994, art: Dave Johnson)

'The Murders On The Rue Morgue' (Issue 13, July 1994, art: Neil Gaiman)

'Fires I Wish I'd Seen' (Issue 14, August 1994, art: Colleen Doran)

'Madame October' (Issue 16, October 1994, art: Terry Moore)

'The Hair Of The Snake That Bit Me' (Issue 17, November 1994, art: Bill Koeb)

'Trampling Tokyo' (Issue 18, December 1994, art: Arthur Adams)

'Litvinov's Book' (Issue 19, January 1995, art: Richard Pace)

'Chiaroscuro' (Issue 25, July 1995, art: Dave Gibbons)

'Me And Dorothy Parker' (Issue 26, August 1995, art: Michael Gaydos)

'Rose Madder' (Issue 28, October 1995, art: James Owen)

'Leopard Man At C&As' (Issue 35, May 1996, art: Jordan Raskin)
'Town Of Lights' (Issue 37, July 1996, art: Mark Rickets)
Issue 15 has Moore's name on the cover, but nothing from him inside.
Alan Moore's Songbook (October 1998) collected all the above, except for 'Another Suburban Romance' and 'Town Of Lights.' 'Positively Bridge Street' was also reprinted in *Best Of Negative Burn* (1995).

Batman

Moore wrote a five-page text story, 'The Gun,' for the British *Batman Annual* 1985 (Autumn 1984, art: Garry Leach).

In the US, he contributed the story 'Mortal Clay' to *Batman Annual* 11 (April 1987, art: George Freeman). While Batman also makes appearances in a number of Moore's Superman and Swamp Thing stories (*Swamp Thing* 53 being a fully-fledged crossover), his most significant Batman story is *Batman: The Killing Joke* (May 1988, art: Brian Bolland). *The Killing Joke* has remained in print since its first release. In 1990 it was translated into French as *Batman: Souriez!* (trans: Julien Grycan), which is resized and slightly edited to fit a paperback format.

Big Numbers

One of Moore's great unfinished projects. Twelve issues of *Big Numbers* were planned, but only two issues appeared: Issue 1 in April 1990, Issue 2 in August the same year (art: Bill Sienkiewicz).

The Bojeffries Saga

The Bojeffries Saga starts in *Warrior* 12 (August 1983, art: Steve Parkhouse), with 'The Rentman Cometh.' 'One Of Our Rentmen Is Missing' was in the following issue (13, October 1983), with the two-part 'Raoul's Night Out' appearing in issues 19-20 (June-July 1984). These were reprinted, colourised, in *Flesh and Bones* 1-4 (1986). As a preface to that, the new story 'Batfishing In Suburbia' appeared in *Dalgoda* 8 (April 1986, four pages).

New instalments followed in *A1*: 'Festus: Dawn Of The Dead' in issue 1 (May 1989), 'Sex With Ginda Bojeffries' (2, September 1989), 'A Quiet Christmas With The Family' (3, February 1990), 'Song Of The Terraces'

(4, April 1990) and 'Our Factory Fortnight' in *The A1 True Life Bikini Confidential* (February 1991).

This material was collected and colourised for *The Complete Bojeffries Saga* (1992), along with some previously unseen material: 'Under The Settee With Len,' '4-Dimensional Fenestrations,' 'Festus: Hallowe'en Masque,' 'Ginda's Fabulous Fashions' and 'Raoul's Recipe.'

Captain Britain

Moore started writing the Captain Britain strip from *Marvel Superheroes* 387 (July 1982, art: Alan Davies). After one more issue (388, August 1982), the story transferred to *The Daredevils*, where it appeared in all issues (January-November 1983). That title merged with *The Mighty World Of Marvel*, and the *Captain Britain* strip runs from issue 7 (December 1983). Moore continued to write the strip until issue 13 (June 1984).

In 1995, Marvel UK produced *X-Men Archives*, a seven-part series that reprints the early Captain Britain strips in the American comic book format, but with a great amount of care going into the resizing and colouring. Moore's scripts start in issue 2 (August 1995), issue 7 (January 1996) ends with Moore's last instalment.

DC Comics

Moore wrote some substantial work for DC Comics: *Swamp Thing*, *V For Vendetta*, *Watchmen*, and also significant stories for Superman and Batman. Each of those warrants a separate entry. He also wrote a number of back-up and one-off stories:

Detective Comics 549-550 (April-May 1985, art: Klaus Janson). A two part Green Arrow back-up strip 'Night Olympics' (seven pages per part).

Vega back-up strips in *Omega Men* 26 ('Brief Lives,' April 1985, art: Kevin O'Neill) and issue 27 ('A Man's World,' May 1985, art: Paris Cullins).

Vigilante 17-18 (May-June 1985, art: Jim Baikie). A two-part (full-length) story 'Father's Day.'

Green Lantern 188 (May 1985, art: Dave Gibbons). A Green Lantern Corps back-up strip 'Mogo Doesn't Socialize.'

Tales Of The Green Lantern Corps Annual 2 (1986, art: Kevin O'Neill), 12-page strip 'Tygers.' Annual 3 (1987, art: Bill Willingham), 6-page story 'In Blackest Night.'

Secret Origins issue 10 (January 1987, 10 pages, art: Joe Orlando), one of several possible origin stories for the Phantom Stranger, 'Footsteps.'

Doctor Who

Moore wrote a number of back-up strips for *Doctor Who Weekly* (which became *Doctor Who Monthly* with issue 44) featuring monsters from *Doctor Who*, but not the Doctor himself: the Cybermen in 'Black Legacy' (35-38, June-July 1980, art: David Lloyd), the Autons in 'Business As Usual' (40-43, July-August 1980, art: David Lloyd, reprinted in the *Doctor Who Summer Special 1981*), and the early Time Lords in 'Star Death,' (47, December 1980, art: John Stokes); '4-D War' (51, April 1981, art: David Lloyd), 'Black Sun Rising' (57, October 1981, art: David Lloyd).

Most back-up stories in *Doctor Who Weekly* were written by Steve Moore, and credits for just 'Moore' have caused a number of misattributions over the years.

To coincide with the arrival of the Special Executive in Captain Britain, their first appearance in the Time Lord strips were reprinted, slightly edited to downplay the link to Doctor Who, in *The Daredevils* issues 5-7 (May-July 1983). Issue 5 also has a text page from Moore re-introducing his creations.

The American *Doctor Who* comic reprinted colourised versions of 'Black Legacy' in issue 14 (November 1985) and 'Business As Usual' in issue 15 (January 1986).

D.R. & Quinch

D.R. and Quinch started life in a one-off *Time Twister* in *2000AD* 317 ('D.R. & Quinch Have Fun On Earth,' credited to EE Quinch, May 1983, art: Alan Davis). They returned in their own series to 'Go Straight' in 350 – 351, 'Go Girl Crazy!' (352-354) and 'Get Drafted' (355-359) between January and March 1984, returning the following month to 'Go To Hollywood' (364-367). The *2000AD Sci-Fi Special 1985* has the six-page 'D.R & Quinch Get Back To Nature.'

Issue 450 (December 1985) has a D.R. & Quinch Christmas cover, by Davis, but no strip inside. In 1987, the characters would appear in an 'Agony Page,' but this was written by Jamie Delano, not Moore.

The strips were resized and recoloured for the American market in *2000AD Monthly* 1-5 (April-Aug 1985), which reprinted issues 350-359. *The Best of 2000AD Monthly* 6-8 and 17-19 saw a British reprint of the complete adventures in their original format. They were collected in the trade paperback *D.R. & Quinch's Totally Awesome Guide To Life* (October 1986, with an introduction by Moore). Five years later the same material (minus the introduction) was colourised again (and a better job was made of it) and released as *Definitive Editions: D.R. & Quinch* (August 1991). A new black and white collected edition appeared in November 2001.

Extreme Studios/Awesome

Moore's revamp of *Supreme* begins with issue 41 (August 1996, art: Joe Bennett/Norm Rapmund and a flashback sequence by Keith Giffen/Al Gordon). Rick Veitch started doing the flashback sequences with the next issue (42, September 1996). Dan Jurgens and Rapmund drew Omniman sequences for issue 43 (October 1996, now under the Maximum Press banner). Richard Horie was penciller for issue 44 (January 1997). J Morrigan was penciller for issues 46 and 47 (February-March 1997), along with Bennett/Rapmund and Veitch). Mark Pajarillo joined Rapmund for the first Awesome issue 49 (June 1997) and 50 (July 1997). Issue 51 appeared in August, and three issues came out in September - 52A, 52B and 53 (52A includes an eight-page strip by Kevin O'Neill). New regular artist Chris Sprouse (inked by Al Gordon) starts with the last of those (although guests still do small flashback or other homage sequences – Melinda Gebbie in 54, November 1997; Gil Kane in 55, December 1997). However, the series abruptly ceased publication with issue 56 (February 1998). Despite the new title and numbering, and the gap of over a year, *Supreme: The Return* 1 (April 1999) used the material originally intended for issue 57 of *Supreme*. The series continued to appear sporadically and (as Sprouse was now working on *Tom Strong* for Moore, see 'ABC') with a variety of artists: 2 (June 1999, art: Jim Starlin), 3 (November 1999, art: Matt Smith, Rick Veitch, Jim Baikie, Al Gordon, Rob Liefeld), 4 (March 2000, art: Matt Smith, Rick Veitch), 5 (May 2000, art: Ian Churchill, Rick Veitch/Norm Rapmund), and the last issue to date, 6 (March 2000, art: Rick Veitch & Rob Liefeld). Moore originally completed scripts for *Supreme* 57 – 64, meaning that there are now just two issues of Supreme material, the two-part 'The Clash Of The Supremacies,' left to publish.

Issues 41 and 42 were reprinted together as the *Supreme: Collected Edition* (April 1997).

The crossover event *Judgment Day* came in three parts, *Alpha* (June 1997, art: Rob Liefeld, Gil Kane, Stephen Platt, Joe Weems V, Keith Giffen, Bill Wray, Adam Pollina, Jon Sibal, Dan Jurgens, Al Gordon), *Omega* (July 1997, art: Rob Liefeld, Chris Sprouse, Al Gordon, Steve Skroce, Stephen Platt, Lary Stucker, Jim Starlin, Alan Weiss, Terry & Rachel Dodson) and *Final Judgment* (November 1997, art: Rob Liefeld, Mara Mychaels, Cedric Nocon, Jon Siba, Lary Stucker, Norm Rapmund, Jeff Johnson, Dan Panosian, Rick Veitch, Ian Churchill). This was followed by *Judgment Day: Aftermath* (March 1998, art: Gil Kanc & Marlo Alquiza). The *Judgment Day Sourcebook* (1997, art: Chris Sprouse & Al Gordon) includes a new six-page prologue and prints some of Moore's notes about the series and characters.

'Youngblood Prologue Featuring Shaft' (art: Steve Skroce & Lary Stucker appears in both the *Youngblood Special Exclusive Edition* 1+ (December 1997) and the *Awesome Holiday Special* (December 1997). The series proper starts with *Youngblood* 1 (February 1998) but it would be August (1998) before the second issue arrived. That was the last issue, although the story continues in *Awesome Adventures* 1 (August 1999) in material originally intended for issue 3. Moore apparently wrote (or at least had completed synopses for) another three issues.

The only Glory solo story to see the light of day to date is the eight-page 'Glory And The Gate Of Tears' (art: Brandon Peterson & Edwin Rosell), which first appeared in 1998, in a *Glory/Re-gex* convention preview, in black and white. The story, in colour, with a couple of pages resized to become double-page spreads (bringing it to 10 pages), along with sketchbook appeared as *Glory* 0 (March 1999). Moore is reported to have written *Glory* scripts for either two or three full issues, and had plotted out around half a dozen more in at least some form. Avatar Press have announced they will print these as a four-part mini-series in 2002. A new *Glory Preview* appeared in October 2001, including five previously unseen pages 'Gates of Dawn, Chapter 1 : The Seventh Dagger' (art: Marat Mychaels).

A *Warchild* maxi-series was announced but never released.

Awesome Adventures was meant to be a monthly series and the intention seemed to be to print Moore's unpublished *Youngblood*, *Glory* and *Warchild* work there. As it was, only the first issue was published.

Alan Moore's Awesome Universe Handbook contains notes by Moore outlining his thoughts on *Glory* and *Youngblood*, along with concept sketches by Alex Ross (April 1999). A second volume was planned dealing with *Warchild* and *The Allies*, but has never appeared.

From Hell

The prologue originally appears in *Cerebus* 124 (July 1989, eight pages, art: Eddie Campbell), a lead-in to the run in *Taboo* which printed the first six chapters in issues 2 (1989), 3 (1989), 4 (1990), 5 (1991), 6 (1992) and 7 (1992). Early chapters were reprinted in their own title from March 1991 with the addition of detailed appendices which would be a feature of every issue. When *Taboo* folded, new material was published in *From Hell* from issue 4 (March 1994), and the series continued in 5 (June 1994), 6 (November 1994), 7 (April 1995), 8 (July 1995), 9 (April 1996), 10 (August 1996) and an epilogue, *From Hell: Dance Of The Gull-Catchers* (September 1998).

The series was collected into a trade paperback (November 1999). There was also a limited edition (1000 copies) hardcover.

The full scripts of the prologue and the first three chapters were printed (along with sketches from Campbell) as *From Hell: The Compleat Scripts* (1994). This was the first of four planned volumes, but a contractual clash with the movie has prevented any follow-ups.

The Ballad Of Halo Jones

Book One originally appeared in *2000AD* 376-385 (July-September 1984, art: Ian Gibson), Book Two in 405-415 (February-April 1985) and Book Three in 451-466 (January-April 1985).

The stories were reprinted in *The Best Of 2000AD Monthly* (Book One in issue 40, January 1989; Book Two in issue 42, March 1989; Book Three in issues 65-66, February-March 1991), which also included black and white reprints of supplementary material like covers and posters.

The first instalment of Book One was reprinted in a mini-comic with a new Halo Jones poster by Gibson bound into *2000AD* issue 725 (April 1991).

Quality Comics resized and colourised the story for the American market, which ran as *Halo Jones* issues 1-12, (September 1987-August 1988). Shrinking the artwork rendered it all but unintelligible, and crudely colouring it finished the job.

Titan Books reprinted trade paperback editions, *The Ballad Of Halo Jones*, Books One to Three (August-October 1986), with introductions by Moore, reproductions of covers and posters, as well as sketchbook material. In September 1991, Titan published *The Complete Halo Jones*, with a new introduction by Moore. A new edition was issued in July 2001 reprinting the three original introductions but without the sketchbook material, the covers or posters.

Image Comics

The *1963* mini-series appeared as six books *Mystery Incorporated* (April 1993, art: Rick Veitch & Dave Gibbons), *The Fury* (May 1993, art: Veitch & Stephen Bissette), *Tales Of The Uncanny* (June 1993, art: Bissette & Veitch), *Tales From Beyond* (July 1993, art: Bissette & Totleben, Jim Valentino & Bissette), *Horus – Lord Of Light* (August 1993, art: Veitch & Totleben), *The Tomorrow Syndicate* (October 1993, art: Veitch & Gibbons). The story was meant to end in a Double Image 80-Page Giant, but this was never published.

A Horus – Lord of Light story appeared in *Hero Premiere* 6 (eight pages, art: Veitch & Totleben).

Moore was guest writer for *Spawn* 8 (March 1993, art: Todd McFarlane, reprinted in *Spawn: Book Two*, August 1997) and *Spawn* 37 (November 1995, art: Greg Capullo).

Moore wrote four mini-series using characters from *Spawn*: *Violator* 1 – 3 (May – July 1994, art: Bart Sears (1-2), Greg Capullo 3); *Violator/ Badrock* 1-4 (May-August 1995, art: Brian Denham); *Spawn: Blood Feud* 1-4 (June-September 1995, art: Tony Daniel, Kevin Conrad) and *Spawn/ WildC.A.T.S.* 1-4 (January-April 1996, art: Scott Clark, Sal Regla).

There was a ten-page story, 'Shadows In The Sand' in *Shadowhawks Of Legend* (December 1995, art: Steve Leialoha), and Moore supplied 'swell dialogue' for *The Maxx* 21 (January 1996, art: Sam Kieth).

Lost Girls

Another incomplete work, the first six chapters of *Lost Girls* (art: Melinda Gebbie) appeared in *Taboo* 5-7 (1991-1992). These were reprinted in *Lost Girls* Book One (November 1995), along with sketchbook material, and Book Two (February 1996), which also included the previously unpublished Chapter Seven.

Top Shelf have announced a lavish three-book hardcover slipcase edition of the complete *Lost Girls* for release in late 2001, which will run to 240 pages (compared to the 56 pages published so far).

Marvelman/Miracleman

Moore's Marvelman first appears in *Warrior*, starting in issue 1 (March 1982, art: Garry Leach) and continuing until issue 21 (August 1984, art: Alan Davis from issue 6 onwards). There is no *Marvelman* strip in issue 19. Instead of the regular *Marvelman* in issue 12, there is an untitled *Young Marvelman* strip, and in issue 17 there's a *Marvelman Family* story, 'The Red King Syndrome' (art: John Ridgway in both cases).

One chapter that appears in *Warrior*, 'The Yesterday Gambit' (Issue 4, Summer Special 1982, art: Steve Dillon), is a flash-forward to the end of the series and has never been reprinted.

The American series *Miracleman* issue 1 (August 1985) has resized and colourised reprints of the *Warrior* material (the first issue includes a reprinted fifties strip with new dialogue). New material starts halfway through issue 6 (February 1986) with art by Chuck Beckum (issues 6-7), Rick Veitch (issues 9-10) and John Totleben (issues 11-16). Moore's run ends with issue 16 (December 1989). 'The Red King Syndrome' is reprinted in two parts in *Miracleman* 4 and 5, and the untitled *Young Marvelman* strip is in issue 6, both resized and colourised. Issue 8 is a filler issue, featuring reprinted fifties strips, and no material from Moore, and so doesn't appear in the collected reprint of the run.

The one-shot *Marvelman Special* reprints fifties Marvelman strips with framing material by Moore linking it back to the story running in *Warrior* (May 1984, art: Alan Davis). There is a slightly re-edited, resized American reprint, *Miracleman Special 3D* (December 1985), which also came in a non-3D (colourised) version.

Three *Miracleman* books collect the series as they were published in the United States. These are *A Dream Of Flying* (issues 1-3, October 1988), *The Red King Syndrome* (issues 4-7, 9-10, July 1990) and *Olympus* (issues 11-16, December 1990). All three were issued in hardback as well as trade paperback editions. There was a French edition of the first volume (trans: Alain Clément) and a Portugeuse version of the first volume. *Kimota: The Miracleman Companion* (September 2001) features extensive interviews with everyone involved with the Marvelman revival, including Moore, and reprints the first script and Moore's original pitch for the series as well as sketchbook material..

Maxwell The Magic Cat

The newspaper strip appeared in the *Northants Post* from 25 August 1979 to 9 October 1986. All the strips were reprinted in four *Maxwell The Magic Cat* volumes by Acme Press (1986-1987), which also include background articles, a star-studded Maxwell gallery and, in the first volume, an afterword from Moore. Some strips were also reprinted in *The Most Splat* 2 (March 1987), *Speakeasy* (1987-1988), *Kimota* 3 (Winter 1995) and *Strip Aids* (1996).

Skizz

The story originally ran in *2000AD* 308-330 (March-August 1983, art: Jim Baikie).

It was reprinted and colourised in *2000AD Presents* 1-8 (April-November 1986), and again in *Skizz: First Encounter* 1-3 (1988).

Skizz was collected as a trade paperback, with a new introduction by Baikie (March 1989, Titan Books).

Star Wars

Moore wrote short strips for Marvel UK's *Empire Strikes Back Monthly*: 'The Pandora Effect' (issue 151, November 1981, art: Adolfo Buyalla, reprinted in the *Star Wars Summer Special* 1983); 'Tilotny Throws A Shape' (issue 154, August 1982, art: John Stokes); 'Dark Lord's Conscience' (issue 155, April 1982, art: John Stokes); 'Rust Never Sleeps' (issue 156, May 1982, art: Alan Davis); 'Blind Fury' (issue 159, March 1982, art: John Stokes). Colourised reprints were collected by Dark Horse in the two-part series *Classic Star Wars: Devilworlds* (August-September 1996). Alongside 'Dark Lord's Conscience' and 'Blind Fury,' issue 1 also includes reprints of stories by Steve Moore and Steve Parkhouse. Issue 2 contains just the other three Moore stories.

Superman

Alan Moore's earliest published Superman stories are text stories in UK annuals. *The Superheroes Annual* 1984 (Autumn 1983) has a two page story, 'Protected Species,' illustrated by Bryan Talbot. *Superman*

Annual 1985 (Autumn 1984) includes the four page 'I Was Superman's Double,' illustrated by Bob Wakelin.

More substantial is the work he did for DC in the United States:

'For the Man Who Has Everything' first appeared in *Superman Annual* 11 (June 1985, art: Dave Gibbons). It was reprinted in the trade paperback *The Greatest Superman Stories Ever Told* (1987) as well as serialised in the British *Superman* comic (1988).

DC Comics Presents 85 (September 1985, art: Rick Veitch) is a Swamp Thing/Superman crossover.

'Whatever Happened To The Man Of Tomorrow?' appeared originally in two parts, *Superman* 423 and *Action Comics* 583 (September 1986, art: Curt Swan, George Perez). The story was collected in *Superman: Whatever Happened To The Man Of Tomorrow?* (December 1996).

All Moore's Superman comic strips were collected (in black and white) in the trade paperback *Superman: The Man Of Tomorrow* (May 1988).

Swamp Thing

Moore's run on *The Saga Of The Swamp Thing* starts with issue 20 (January 1984, art: Dan Day, John Totleben). The art is by Stephen Bissette and Totleben from issue 21 to 29. The title changes to just *Swamp Thing* with issue 30 (December 1984), and from there Bissette and Totleben and other artists (Alfredo Alcala, Ron Randall, Rick Veitch and Stan Woch) work on the series in a variety of combinations. Shawn McManus is the guest artist for issue 32. Moore doesn't write issue 59 (although he is credited on the cover) or issue 62. His final issue is 64 (September 1987).

Moore wrote one *Swamp Thing* Annual (Annual 2, January 1985, art: Stephen Bissette, John Totleben), which follows on from issue 31.

In America, DC have released trade paperback editions that collect this material – *Saga Of The Swamp Thing* (Issues 21-27, September 1987, with a foreword by Ramsay Campbell and a new seven-page introduction by Moore), *Love and Death* (Issues 28-34 and *Swamp Thing Annual* 2, November 1990), *The Curse* (Issues 35-42, December 2000) and *A Murder of Crows* (Issues 43-50, 2001), and there are plans for trade paperbacks of the remainder of the run. *Swamp Thing* issues 21-43 and *Swamp Thing Annual* 2 are reprinted in black and white comics as *Essential Vertigo: Swamp Thing* (24 issues, September 1996-August 1998). The reprint of Annual 2 is in issue 12. Issue 21 was reprinted in colour as *Millennium Edition: Swamp Thing 21* (September 2000).

In the UK, Titan reprinted issues 21 to 64 in eleven black and white *Swamp Thing* trade paperbacks (April 1987-March 1989). Volume One has an introduction by James Herbert, Volume Two by Clive Barker. Annual 2 is reprinted as part of Volume 7.

Moore also wrote a Swamp Thing/Superman crossover for *DC Comics Presents* 85 (September 1985, art: Rick Veitch), see the entry for 'Superman.'

One curio is *DC Sampler* 2 (September 1984), which includes a text piece by Moore with an illustration by Bissette and Totleben. These are reprinted on the back cover of *The Saga Of The Swamp Thing* paperback. A more straightforward three-page strip/advert appears in *DC Sampler* issue 3 (1984). There is a short interview with Moore about Swamp Thing in *DC Spotlight* issue 1 (1985), as well as a slightly longer piece about *Watchmen*.

2000AD

As well as the running series he wrote for *2000AD* (*D.R. & Quinch*, *The Ballad of Halo Jones* and *Skizz* – see individual entries), Moore supplied a large number of one-off strips, often under the Future Shocks, Time Twisters and Ro-Jaws Robo-Tales banners. Some of these are uncredited or published under pseudonyms – where known, these are noted. The *2000AD Winter Special 1990* has an index of one-off strips, and so represents the best authority on the subject.

The stories are listed by title, the issue of *2000AD* they appeared in and are in order of publication.

'A Holiday In Hell' (*2000AD Sci-Fi Special 1980*, June 1980, art: Dave Harwood)

'The Killer In The Cab' (170, July 1980, art: John Richardson, reprinted in *2000AD* 532)

'The Dating Game' (176, August 1980, art: Dave Gibbons, reprinted: *Spellbinders* 7)

'Final Solution' (189-190, December 1980, art: Steve Dillon, reprinted: *Twisted Times*)

'Grawks Bearing Gifts' (203, March 1981, art: 'Q Twerk' (Ian Gibson), reprinted: *Shocking Futures*, *Strontium Dog Special* 1)

'The Return Of The Two-Storey Brain' (209, April 1981, art: Mike White, reprinted: *Time Twisters* 7 – but very specifically not reprinted in *Twisted Tales* as Moore felt he'd plagiarised the story)

'The English Phlondrutian Phrasebook' (214, May 1981, art: Brendan McCarthy, reprinted: *Shocking Futures*, *Time Twisters* 1)

'The Last Rumble Of The Platinum Horde' (217, June 1981, art: John Higgins, reprinted: *Shocking Futures*, *666 Mark of the Beast* 13, *Time Twisters* 1)

'They Sweep The Spaceways' (219, July 1981, art: Garry Leach, reprinted: *Shocking Futures*, *Time Twisters* 1)

'Ro-Busters: Bax the Burner' (*2000AD* Annual 1982, August 1981, art: Steve Dillon, reprinted: *Sam Slade: Robohunter* 6, *Cyber Crush* 14)

'The Regrettable Ruse Of Rocket Redglare' (234, October 1981, art: Mike White, reprinted: *Shocking Futures*, *Time Twisters* 8)

'The Double Decker Dome Strikes Back' (237-238, November 1981, art: Mike White, reprinted: *Twisted Times*, *Halo Jones* 7)

'A Cautionary Fable' (240, November 1981, art: Paul Neary, reprinted: *Shocking Futures*, *Strontium Dog* 4)

'Mister Could You Use A Squonge?' (mistakenly attributed to Kelvin Gosnell in the *Winter Special* list – 242, December 1981, art: Ron Tiner, reprinted: *Time Twisters* 1)

'Halfway To Paradise' (245, January 1982, art: John Cooper, reprinted: *Twisted Times*, *Halo Jones* 8)

'A Second Chance' (245, January 1982, art: Jose Casanovas, reprinted: *Time Twisters* 1)

'Twist Ending' (246, January 1982, art: Paul Neary, reprinted: *Time Twisters* 7)

'Salad Days!' (247, January 1982, art: John Higgins, reprinted: *Time Twisters* 3)

'The Beastly Beliefs Of Benjamin Blint' (249, January 1982, art: Eric Bradbury, reprinted: *Time Twisters* 7)

'All Of Them Were Empty' (251, February 1982, art: Paul Neary, reprinted: *Time Twisters* 3)

'An American Werewolf In Space' (252, February 1982, art: Paul Neary, reprinted: *Shocking Futures*, *Time Twisters* 1)

'Bounty Hunters' (253, February 1982, art: John Higgins, reprinted: *Strontium Dog* 1)

'The Multistorey Mind Mellows Out!' (254, March 1982, art: Paul Neary, reprinted: *Twisted Times*)

'Wages Of Sin' (257, March 1982, art: Bryan Talbot, reprinted: *Shocking Futures*, *Time Twisters* 3)

'Return Of The Thing' (265, May 1982, art: Dave Gibbons)

'Skirmish' (267, June 1982, art: Dave Gibbons, reprinted: *Time Twisters* 8)

'The Writing On The Wall' (268, June 1982, art: Jesus Redondo, reprinted: *Time Twisters* 9)

'The Wild Frontier' (269, June 1982, art: Dave Gibbons, reprinted: *Shocking Futures, Time Twisters* 1)

'The Big Day' (270, June 1982, art: Robin Smith)

'One Christmas During Eternity' (271, July 1982, art: Jesus Redondo, reprinted: *Shocking Futures, Time Twisters* 9)

'No Picnic' (272, July 1982, art: John Higgins)

'The Disturbed Digestions Of Doctor Dibworthy' (273, July 1982, art: Dave Gibbons, reprinted: *Twisted Times, Time Twisters* 2)

'Hot Item' (278, August 1982, art: John Higgins)

'Ro-Busters: Old Red Eyes Is Back' (*2000AD* Annual 1983, August 1982, art: Bryan Talbot)

'Pray For War' (*2000AD* Annual 1983, August 1982, art: Brett Ewins, reprinted: *Rogue Trooper* 7)

'Sunburn' (282, September 1982, art: Jesus Redondo, reprinted: *Shocking Futures, 666 Mark Of The Beast* 13, *Halo Jones* 1)

'Bad Timing' (291, November 1982, art: Mike White, reprinted: *Shocking Futures, Time Twisters* 4)

'Genius Is Pain' (299, January 1983, art: Mike White, reprinted: *Twisted Times*, Halo Jones 9)

'The Reversible Man' (308, March 1983, art: Mike White, reprinted: *Twisted Times, 666 Mark Of The Beast* 13)

'Einstein' (untitled, but this title appears in the Winter Special list - 309, Mar 83, art: John Higgins, reprinted: *Time Twisters* 4)

'Chronocops' (310, April 1983, art: Dave Gibbons, reprinted: *Twisted Times*)

'The Big Clock' (315, May 1983, art: Eric Bradbury, reprinted: *Time Twisters* 9)

'Doctor Dibworthy's Disappointing Day' (316, May 1983, art: Alan Langford, reprinted: *Time Twisters* 6)

'D.R. & Quinch Have Fun On Earth' (credited to EE Quinch - 317, May 1983, art: Alan Davis, see separate entry for *D.R. & Quinch*).

'Going Native' (318, May 1983, art: Mike White, reprinted: *Time Twisters* 21)

'Ring Road' (320, June 1983, art: Jesus Redondo, reprinted: *Twisted Times, 666: Mark Of The Beast* 12, *Time Twisters* 7)

'The Hyper Historical Headbang' (322, June 1983, art: Alan Davis, reprinted: *Shocking Futures*, *Time Twisters* 1)

'The Lethal Laziness Of Lobelia Loam' (uncredited - 323, July 1983, art: Arturo Boluda, reprinted: *Shocking Futures*)

'The Time Machine' (324, July 1983, art: Jesus Redondo, reprinted: *Twisted Times*, *Time Twisters* 2)

'Eureka' (325, July 1983, art: Mike White, reprinted: *Shocking Futures*, *Time Twisters* 8)

'The Startling Success Of Sideways Scuttleton' (327, July 1983, art: John Higgins)

'Dad' (329, August 1983, art: Alan Langford)

'Buzz Off' (331, August 1983, art: Jim Eldridge)

'First Of The Few' (*2000AD* Annual 1984, August 1983, art: Jesus Redondo, reprinted: *Rogue Trooper* 47, *2000AD Winter Special* 1)

'Storm Eagles Are Go' (*2000AD* Annual 1984, August 1983, art: Joe Eckers)

'Look Before You Leap' (332, August 1983, art: Mike White)

'Red Planet Blues' (*2000AD* Annual 1985, August 1984, art: Steve Dillon)

'Tharg's Head Revisited' (500, December 1986, art: Ian Gibson, single page of anniversary story, reprinted: *Time Twisters* 2)

Many of the strips (as noted) were reprinted, resized and colourised in various American titles: *Cyber Crush, Halo Jones, Judge Dredd Classics, Rogue Trooper, Sam Slade: Robohunter, 666: Mark Of The Beast, Spellbinders, Strontium Dog* and *Time Twisters*.

Alan Moore's Shocking Futures (November 1986) and *Alan Moore's Twisted Times* (January 1987) were trade paperback collections of what Moore considered to be the best of this work (as noted), with new introductions by Moore explaining his choices.

V For Vendetta

Like *Marvelman, V For Vendetta* started life in the first issue of *Warrior* (March 1982, art: David Lloyd) and appeared in every issue until the last, issue 26 (February 1985). Issue 5 had an additional five-page V story, 'Vertigo.' Issue 12 replaced the regular storyline with a comic strip version of the song *This Vicious Cabaret* (a fold-out version was issued with the single). Instead of the strip in issue 17, Moore wrote a long article explaining the genesis of the series, which is reprinted at the back of the collected edition. The regular storyline was also interrupted in issue 20 with the four-page story 'Vincent' (art: Tony Weare, written by David Lloyd).

DC's ten-part *V For Vendetta* (September 1988-May 1989) had colourised reprints of all the *Warrior* strips until issue 7, which then continued with new material. DC collected it in one trade paperback volume and included Moore's article from *Warrior* 17.

There is also a six-volume French edition (1988-1989) *V Pour Vendetta* and a four-part German edition *V Wie Vendetta* (trans: by Carlsen Verlag).

Watchmen

Originally released as the twelve-part series *Watchmen* (September 1986-October 1987, art: Dave Gibbons), the story was collected in one trade paperback, which was first issued almost as soon as the series was complete (December 1987).

DC and Graphitti Designs also issued a leather-bound, slipcase hardback edition in 1988, which reprinted the series and also included forty pages of sketches, background notes and extracts from scripts. It was announced as a limited edition of fifteen thousand, but it's thought that less than two hundred copies of this were actually made.

The first issue was reprinted in January 2000 as part of a range of seminal DC Comics as *Millennium Edition: Watchmen* 1 (January 2000).

There are also editions in both French (*Les Gardiens*, six parts, trans: Jean-Patrick Manchette, September 1987-November 1988) and German (*Der Watcher*, twelve parts, 1988).

Wildstorm

Moore's run on *WildC.A.T.S.* begins with issue 21 of the Image title (July 1995), and continues until issue 34 (February 1997). There is a bewildering number of pencillers: Travis Charest (21, 25-31); Kevin Maguire (22); Ryan Benjamin (23-24, 29-30); Jason Johnson (23-24); Dave Johnson (25-28); Kevin Nowlan (25); Scott Clark (27); Aron Wiesenfeld (28); Jim Lee (31-32); Josh Wiesenfeld (31); Richard Bennett (31); Mat Broome (32-34); Pat Lee (32) and Rob Stotz (34). Not to mention an extraordinary array of inkers: Troy Hubbs (21-22, 25, 33-34); Randy Elliot (22); Sal Regla (22, 30); Trevor Scott (22, 32, 34); Scott Williams (22, 26); Art Thibert (23); Hkjoon Kang (23); Andy Owens (23);

Harry Thuran (23); Terry Austin (23); Tom McWeeny (24); Kevin Nowlan (25); John Nyberg (25); JD (26, 28, 29, 34); Dave Johnson (26, 28); Bob Wiacek (27); Dexter Vines (27); Richard Friend (29-30); Mark Irwin (29-30); Sandra Hope (30, 34); John Tighe (30); Luke Rizzo (30); Richard Bennett (32); Jason Gorder (32) and Scott Taylor (33, 34).

Moore returned to write the last eight pages of the last Image issue, 50 (June 1998, art: Charest & JD).

Moore's run on the series was collected in two trade paperbacks, *WildC.A.T.S: Homecoming* (Issues 21-27, August 1998) and *WildC.A.T.S: Gang War* (28-34, May 1999).

Fire From Heaven was a two-part mini-series, the focus for a crossover event linking a number of Image titles (including *WildC.A.T.S.)*. Issue 1 (March 1996) had art by Ryan Benjamin and Chuck Gibson, issue 2 (July 1996) by Jim Lee. Both are credited to Moore, but neither read like his work – a number of sources state that Warren Ellis wrote the second issue.

'Majestic: The Big Chill' appeared in *Wildstorm Spotlight* 1 (February 1997, art: Carlos d'Anda) and is reprinted in the *Mr Majestic* collected edition (February 2002).

He also wrote the *Spawn/WildC.A.T.S* crossover series (see 'Image').

There were also two mini-series: *Voodoo* 1-4 (November 1997-March 1998, dates, art: Mike Lopez (1-2) and Al Rio (2-4)) which was collected as *Voodoo: Dancing In The Dark* (May 1999) and *Deathblow: Byblows* 1-3 (November 1999-January 2000, art: Jim Baikie)

One-offs

(in order of publication)

Around 1971, Moore edited *Embryo*, a xeroxed magazine published by the Northampton Arts Lab, and he contributed poetry and artwork to the title, which ran to at least five issues. One strip written and drawn by Moore, 'Once There Were Demons,' appeared in issue 5 (November 1971).

He contributed one cartoon to another Northampton Arts Lab magazine, *Rovel* (Issue 3, 1971).

Curt Vile wrote 'Anon E Mouse' for the magazine *Anon* around 1977.

The Backstreet Bugle had strips written and drawn by Curt Vile – 'Fat Jap Defamation Funnies' (Issue 10, January 1979) and 'St Pancras Panda' in 16-22 (July-December 1979).

Curt Vile contributed stories to *Dark Star* in 1979 and 1980: 'The Avenging Hunchback' in 19 (March 1979), 'Kultural Krime Komix' in 20

(May 1979), 'Talcum Powder' in 21 (July 1979). Issues 22-25 have 'Three Eyes McGurk And His Death Planet Commandos' (December 1979-December 1980) written by Steve Moore as Pedro Henry and illustrated by Curt Vile, featuring the first appearance of Axel Pressbutton who'd later appear in *Warrior*). Four pages were reprinted in *Rip-Off Comics* 8 (1981 – Moore's first published work in America).

For *Sounds*, always as Curt Vile, Moore wrote *Roscoe Moscow*, 'Who Killed Rock And Roll?', which ran from March 1979 to July 1980. The art for the August 15 1981 instalment was by Savage Pencil. Episode 1 was reprinted in Volume 2 of *Maxwell The Magic Cat*, Episode 26 was reprinted in *Comics Forum* 4. 'The Stars My Degradation' (a continuation of 'Three Eyes McGurk') ran from July 1980 until March 1983. Steve Moore wrote the strip from February 1982 (as Pedro Henry). There were two Christmas stories – 'Christmas On Depravity' (December 1981, reprinted in *Warrior* 16), 'The Bride Of Pressbutton' (December 1982). Moore also wrote and drew 'Ten Little Liggers' (December 1980, four pages) and 'The Rock And Roll Zoo,' August 15 1981, half page).

In 1979 (as Curt Vile) Moore did a sample strip for a proposed series, 'Nutters Ruin.' It wasn't taken up, but saw the light of day in *Speakeasy* 43 and *Maxwell The Magic Cat* Volume 2.

'Scant Applause' in *Frantic Winter Special* 1979 (as Curt Vile, 1979, two pages, art: Moore)

Two photostrips for the new *Eagle* under The Collector banner: 'Trash!' in issue 3 (April 10, 1982, 3½ pages, photography: Sven Arnstein) and 'Profits Of Doom' issue 12 (June 12, 1982, 3½ pages, photography: Gabor Scott, art: Rex Archer).

Not! The World Cup Special 1982 (a spin off from the topical TV comedy *Not The Nine O'Clock News*) had a piece written by Curt Vile and illustrated by Barrie Mitchell.

'Moonstone: Tomorrow's Truths' in *Fantasy Advertiser* 77 (February 1983, art: Mike Collins/Mark Farmer)

'Grit!' A parody of Frank Miller's *Daredevil* appeared in issue 8 of *The Daredevils* (August 1983, art: Mike Collins).

Moore wrote strips featuring the Warpsmiths, characters introduced in *Marvelman* (art: Garry Leach). The two-part 'Cold War, Cold Warrior' appeared in *Warrior* 9-10 (January, May 1983), and as colourised reprint in *Axel Pressbutton* 2 (December 1984). 'Ghostdance' appeared in *A1* 1 (May 1989), clearly intended as the start of a series, but it is not known if Moore wrote any further scripts.

Moore was reportedly the writer of a one-page comic strip advertising the synthetic lubricant Slipstream (uncredited, art: Steve Dillon and John Higgins). It appeared in a number of Marvel UK Comics in late 1983 (e.g. *Doctor Who Monthly* 83).

'Monster' in *Scream!* 1 (March 1984, four pages, art: Heinzl)

Heroes For Hope: Starring The X-Men (December 1985) is a one-shot comic in aid of African Famine relief featuring the work of dozens of writers and artists. Moore wrote pages 16-18 (art: Richard Corben).

'The Riddle Of The Recalcitrant Refuse!' in *Mr Monster* 3 (October 1985, art: Michael T Gilbert, reprinted: *Mr Monster: His Books Of Forbidden Knowledge*, January 1997).

Moore wrote back-up strips for *American Flagg* 21-27 (June 1985-December 1985, art: Larry Stroman). For the conclusion of the story, Moore's strip took up the whole issue.

'Pictopia' (thirteen pages, art: Donald Simpson, Pete Poplaski, Mike Kazaleh) first appeared in *Anything Goes!* 2 (December 1986) and was reprinted in *The Best Comics Of The Decade 1980-1990 Volume 1* (June 1990).

'Love Doesn't Last Forever' in *Epic Illustrated* 34 (February 1986, eight pages, art: Rick Veitch)

'Leviticus' in *Outrageous Tales From The Old Testament* (1987, six pages, art: Hunt Emerson)

'Tapestries' in *Real War Stories* issue 1 (July 1987, seven pages, art: Stan Woch & John Totleben (part 1), Stephen Bissette (part 2)).

Two pieces for *Heartbreak Hotel*. Issue 1 (January 1988) artist and writer on 'Letter From Northampton,' single page strip. Issue 3 (March 1988) has 'I Can Hear The Grass Grow' written and illustrated by Curt Vile and an untitled autobiography of Moore.

'The Mirror Of Love' in *AARGH!* (Artists Against Rampant Government Homophobia) (October 1988, eight pages, art: Steve Bissette & Rick Veitch). The text only was reprinted in *Rapid Eye Three* (November 1994).

'Act Of Faith' in *Puma Blues* 20 (1988, four pages, art: Steve Bissette & Michael Zulli)

'Shadowplay: The Secret Team' in *Brought To Light* (January 89, thirty pages, art: Bill Sienkiewicz)

'Lust' in *Seven Deadly Sins* (1989, eight pages, art: Mike Matthews)

'Cold Snap' (art: Bryan Talbot) first appears in *Food For Thought* (April 1985) and is reprinted in *Slow Death* 11 (1992) and in *Ex-Directory, The Secret Files Of Bryan Talbot* (November 1997).

'Come on Down' in *Taboo* 1 (1988, eight pages, art: Bill Wray)

'Bob Wachsman Tummler' in *American Splendor* 15 (May 1990, one page, art: Moore, written by Harvey Pekar).

The graphic novel *A Small Killing* (art: Oscar Zarate) was released in September 1991 in the UK in a hardback and paperback edition. In the US it was released in paperback only in February 1993.

'The Bowing Machine' in *RAW*, volume 2, no 3 (1991, eight pages, art: Mark Beyer)

The Worm: The Longest Comic Strip In The World is the end result of a one day event in the London Trocadero in 1991. It attempted to create a comic strip longer than the Bayeaux Tapestry. Moore supplied a storyline, which was worked into scripts by Jamie Delano, Steve Moore, Andrew Cartmel, Garth Ennis and Hilary Robinson. One hundred and twenty-five artists contributed at least one panel. It was published in book form in 1999.

'Dr Omaha Presents Venus In Fur: Candid Chit-chats With Cartoon Kit-Cats' in *Images Of Omaha* 2 (1992, one page, art: Melinda Gebbie)

'The Nativity On Ice' (as Curt Vile, art: Bryan Talbot) in *Kimota* 3 (Winter 1995)

'I Keep Coming Back' in *It's Dark In London* (1996, twelve pages, art: Oscar Zarate)

'The New European' in *Vampirella/Dracula: The Centennial* (October 1997, twelve pages, art: Gary Frank & Cam Smith). There had been an interview with Moore about Dracula in *Vampirella/Dracula: Showcase* (August 1997, art: Gary Frank).

'Itchy Peterson: Born Lucky I Guess' in *Nightmare Theatre* 4 (October 1997, eight pages, art: Val Semeiks)

Moore wrote four stories for *Will Eisner's The Spirit: The New Adventures*. Three appeared in the first issue, 'The Most Important Meal,' 'Force Of Arms' and 'Gossip And Gertrude Granch' (March 1998, all eight pages, art: Dave Gibbons). The fourth 'Last Night I Dreamt Of Dr Cobra' was in issue 3 (May 1998, ten pages, art: Daniel Torres).

'The Hasty Smear Of My Smile…' appeared in *Hate* 30 (June 1998, four pages, art: Peter Bagge & Eric Reynolds).

'Hungry Is The Heart' in *Meatcake* 9 (April 1999, twelve pages, art: Dame Darcy)

Eddie Campbell did comic strip adaptations of Moore's stage shows *The Birth Caul* (June 1999) and *Snakes And Ladders* (October 2001).

'Lux Brevis' - the pencils (by John Totleben) for the first instalment of this proposed series are printed for the first time in *Kimota: The Miracleman Companion* (September 2001).

Other Stuff

Prose Fiction/Poems

'To The Humfo' in *Weird Windows* 1 (1970) and 'Shrine Of The Lizard' in *Weird Windows* 2 (1971)

As Curt Vile, Moore wrote and illustrated three prose stories for *Sounds*: 'Terror Couple Kill Telegram Sam In The Flat Field' (February 14, 1982, two pages); 'Here Comes The Jetsons' (April 4, 1981, one page); 'Mystery And Abomination' (August 8, 1981, one page).

Nightraven stories ran in *Marvel Superheroes* 391-395 (October 19820-February 1983) and *The Daredevils* 6-10 (June-October 1983). They are illustrated by David Lloyd and Alan Davis.

'Sawdust Memories' in *Knave* (December 1984)

'Brasso With Rosie' in the *Knockabout Trial Special* (1984, one page, art: Peter Bagge, reprinted in *Honk* 2, January 1987)

'Travel Guide For Agoraphobics' (*Honk* 4, March 1987, three pages, illustrated by Eddie Campbell)

The short story 'A Hypothetical Lizard' has appeared in *Liavek: Wizard's Row* (1987), *The Year's Best Fantasy* (1989) and *Words Without Pictures* (1990).

'The Children's Hour' in *Now We Are Sick* (1991)

'The Courtyard' in *The Starry Wisdom: A Tribute To HP Lovecraft* (February 1995)

'Light Of Thy Countenance' in *Forbidden Acts* (October 1995)

Voice Of The Fire, a novel (or at least a short story collection that builds up into a novel), published in 1996.

Moore also contributed a text piece for the *Heroes* comic released as a tribute to firemen and policemen killed in the attack on the World Trade Centre (illustrated by Dave Gibbons, October 2001).

Introductions

Moore has written a number of introductions for comics or trade paperback collections:

Alec McGarry (July 1984)
Escape (Spring 1985)
Doc Chaos (Spring 1985)
The Mechanics 1 (October 1985)
Dark Knight Returns (1986)
Grendel: Devil By The Deed (1986)
Brickman 1 (December 1986)
Violent Cases (1987)
The Adventures Of Luther Arkwright Book Two (December 1987)
The Suttons: Three Years In Maidstone (1988)
Bill Sienkiewicz Sketchbook (1990)
Hellboy: Wake The Devil (1996)
Mr Monster: His Book Of Forbidden Knowledge (January 1997)
Bread And Wine: An Erotic Tale Of New York (March 1999)
Planetary (2000)

Miscellaneous

Ragnarok. Script for a straight-to-video animated anthology of stories, including work by Bryan Talbot. c. 1984.

Outbreak of Violets, card series for MTV Europe, various artists, 1995

Mail. 23. hor. 6. post meridiem. Mortlak. a collage exhibited at the Jago Gallery in Shoreditch (1997)

Illustrations

In 1969, Moore did an illustration for the comic/SF bookshop Dark They Were And Golden Eyed that appeared in *Cyclops*.

NME (1978), illustrations of Elvis Costello and Malcolm McLaren (as Curt Vile).

Illustrations for articles in *Sounds* – October 25 1980 (Cockney Rejects), December 13 1980 (Heavy Metal), June 27 1981 (Bad Manners), August 29 1981 (Mutate and Survive), all as Curt Vile.

Moore supplied one-page pin-ups for *Doc Stearn ... Mr Monster* issues 4 and 5, and the *Mr Monster 3D Triple Threat*.

A one-page drawing in *Godzilla, King Of The Monsters* (August 1987)

Moore supplied covers for *Basil Wolverton's Planet Of Terror!* (October 1987) and *Basil Wolverton's Gateway To Terror* (1987).

The cover of *Prototype* 10 (1994)

Moore contributed to a 'jam' cartoon in *Strip Aids* (1996).

Articles/Essays/Writings

(This lists articles by Moore, rather than ones about him, or interviews with him.)

Moore wrote and illustrated a feature about haunted houses in the *Scooby Doo Annual* 1982.

Sounds: record reviews of *Loud* by Half Japanese in the August 22, 1981 issue, *Mask* by Bauhaus in the issue dated February 26, 1981 (Moore also wrote the sleeve notes for that album, as Brilburn Logue), and a Hawkwind interview 'Wind Power' in the November 11, 1982 issue.

'A Short History Of Britain' in *Marvel Superheroes* 389 (September 1982)

The B.J. And The Bear Annual 1983 has an article and illustrations by Moore.

Moore wrote a number of articles about the state of comics for *The Daredevils*, which ran during 1983. Fanzine reviews appeared in issues 2, 5-8 and 10. There's a six-page article about Frank Miller in issue 1; a two-part Stan Lee article in 3-4. 'O Superman: Music And Comics' in issue 5 (May 1983). Most substantial is a three-part essay on sexism in comics, 'Phantom Ladies And Invisible Girls' which ran in issues 4-6.

'On Writing For Comics' in *Fantasy Advertiser* 92-95 (August 1985-February 1986) revised and reprinted in *Comics Journal* 119-120 (January-March 1988),

'Comments On Crumb' in *Blab* 3 (1988). This may be the same essay that appears in the book *The Life And Times Of R Crumb* (1988).

Comics Forum 4 (Summer 1993) – includes a transcript of a lecture Moore gave to the Preston Speculative Fiction Group, discussing *1963*, feminism, pornography and Image comics among other things.

Comics Journal 167 includes tributes to Jack Kirby from many in the comics industry, including Moore.

'Recognition And Zaman's Hill' in *Dust: A Creation Books Reader* (1995)

Performance Art/Music/CDs

The *V For Vendetta* EP (1984) by David J comprised of 'This Vicious Cabaret' (lyrics by Moore), 'V's Theme' and 'Incidental.' There was a fold-out of the *Warrior* strip with the song's lyrics issued with it. While the EP is impossible to find these days, all three tracks are available on David J's 'best of' album, *On Glass*.

The March Of The Sinister Ducks (1983). Moore (using the alias Translucia Baboon), David J and session saxophonist Alex Green perform a song about ducks and their evil plans. The B-side was 'Old Gangsters Never Die.' The title song was reissued on flexi-disc with *Critters* issue 23 (April 1988) and justified in a two-page prose piece by Moore, 'The True Story Of The Rise And Fall Of The Sinister Ducks.'

Hexentexts: A Creation Books Sampler (December 1991). Moore gives a reading and also drew the cover.

Around 1994 Moore's band The Emperors Of Ice Cream had a demo/compilation tape which wasn't released commercially.

'Me And Dorothy Parker' (1995), a song written by Moore for The Flash Girls (which is adapted for comics in *Negative Burn*).

The Birth Caul: A Shamanism Of Childhood (November 1995) – David J and Tim Perkins joined Moore in an examination of pre-verbal thought and the origin of art and imagination. This was adapted as a comic by Eddie Campbell (see above).

The Moon And Serpent Grand Egyptian Theatre Of Marvels (1996). Moore writes and performs to music by David J.

Brought To Light (May 1998). Moore performs an adaptation of 'Shadowplay: The Secret Team,' music by Gary Lloyd.

Snakes And Ladders (10 April 1999) at Red Lion Square.

The Highbury Working ... A Beat Seance (November 2000). Moore performs poems and stories, encompassing (among other things) the Krays, Coleridge and Pepper's Ghost, to music by Tim Perkins.

Angel Passage (October 2001). Recorded at the 'Tigers Of Wrath' Blake exhibition at the Tate Gallery.

The Essential Library: Currently Available

Film Directors:

Woody Allen (Revised) (£3.99)   Tim Burton (£3.99)
Jane Campion (£2.99)   John Carpenter (£3.99)
Jackie Chan (£2.99)   Joel & Ethan Coen (£3.99)
David Cronenberg (£3.99)   Terry Gilliam (£2.99)
Alfred Hitchcock (£3.99)   Krzysztof Kieslowski (£2.99)
Stanley Kubrick (£2.99)   Sergio Leone (£3.99)
David Lynch (£3.99)   Brian De Palma (£2.99)
Sam Peckinpah (£2.99)   Ridley Scott (£3.99)
Orson Welles (£2.99)   Billy Wilder (£3.99)
Steven Spielberg (£3.99)   Mike Hodges (£3.99)
Ang Lee (£3.99)

Film Genres:

Film Noir (£3.99)   Hong Kong Heroic Bloodshed (£2.99)
Horror Films (£3.99)   Slasher Movies(£3.99)
Spaghetti Westerns (£3.99)   Vampire Films (£2.99)
Blaxploitation Films (£3.99)   Bollywood (£3.99)
French New Wave (£3.99)

Film Subjects:

Laurel & Hardy (£3.99)   Marx Brothers (£3.99)
Steve McQueen (£2.99)   Marilyn Monroe (£3.99)
The Oscars® (£3.99)   Filming On A Microbudget (£3.99)
Bruce Lee (£3.99)   Film Music (£3.99)

TV:

Doctor Who (£3.99)

Literature:

Cyberpunk (£3.99)   Philip K Dick (£3.99)
Agatha Christie (£3.99)   Noir Fiction (£2.99)
Terry Pratchett (£3.99)   Sherlock Holmes (£3.99)
Hitchhiker's Guide (Revised) (£3.99)

Ideas:

Conspiracy Theories (£3.99)   Nietzsche (£3.99)
Feminism (£3.99)

History:

Alchemy & Alchemists (£3.99)   The Crusades (£3.99)
American Civl War (£3.99)   American Indian Wars (£3.99)
The Black Death (£3.99)   Jack The Ripper (£3.99)

Available at all good bookstores, or send a cheque to: **Pocket Essentials (Dept AM), 18 Coleswood Rd, Harpenden, Herts, AL5 1EQ, UK**. Please make cheques payable to 'Oldcastle Books.' Add 50p postage & packing for each book in the UK and £1 elsewhere.